Microsoft in the Mirror

For my parents,
John and Shirley Carter

Acknowledgments

A sincere thank you to Studs Terkel, whose book "Working" sets the standard. I appreciate your interest in my book.

I was helped along the way with advice from Stacia Green, Lesley Link, Cheryl Tsang, Julie Bick, Ted Chiang, Fred Moody, Jharna Jain, Andrew Short, Steve Allen, and Mark Murray.

Monica Harrington, who spent time and care far beyond anything I could have hoped for, Dorcas Kelley, Sonya Stoklosa, Kristin Carter, Mary Trunk—yours was crucial early enthusiasm, Liz Carter, Darl and Chuck Wilson, Heather Newbold, and Tony Pisculli generously read various chapters and gave helpful feedback.

Special thanks for their editing and their encouragement to Caitlin Blasdell and Melanie White.

Artwork by Michael Crosby inspired the image on the cover, and Wendy Green took the photo. Tom Bates, Jerry Davis, and Cathey Rapson participated in a fun evening of brainstorming book titles.

Melanie and Sonya, you kept me going. Thank you! Tom Bates gave endless, patient, loving support and perspective, as always.

Most important of all are the people who tell their stories here. I put this book together the way Tom Sawyer got his fence painted; it wouldn't exist without the contributions of my co-workers.

You amazed me.

Contents

Microsoft
in the Mirror

Nineteen Insiders Reflect on the Experience

Karin Carter

Pennington Books
Redmond, Washington

Microsoft in the Mirror

Published by Pennington Books.

Publisher's Cataloging-in-Publication
(Provided by Quality Books, Inc.)
    Microsoft in the mirror : nineteen insiders reflect on the
    experience / [compiled and edited by] Karin Carter. –
    1st ed.
    p. cm.
    LCCN 2002094979
    ISBN 0-9725299-0-X

    1. Microsoft Corporation—Biography. 2. Computer
software industry—United States—History. I. Carter, Karin.

HD9696.63.U64M5365 2003   338.7'610053'0973
                        QBI02-200742

Cover by Heidi Hackler of Dolphin Design.
Cover photo by Wendy Green.
Printed in the United States of America.

User's Guide

Imagine this: you're an ordinary person, just out of school, living in a shared apartment and driving a battered old car. All you're hoping for is to find work you like that pays the rent. And then, *wham*, you get a job at Microsoft.

Microsoft was my head-spinning world for fourteen years. I landed there by chance and I stayed there because it was an adventure—incredible and hard and frustrating and exciting. Unexpected, too; no stamp saying *Future Winner* appeared under the corporate logo when I joined the company in 1983, and the race to lead the pack never looked like a sure thing. But the place had a magnetic pull.

Our managers often told us that Microsoft's most important asset was its people. It's true. No robotic assembly line creates Microsoft products; they're born in people's minds and come into being through the push and pull of a million meetings and years of work. Who we are had a direct bearing on what Microsoft was, and as the composition of the company changed over the years, Microsoft changed.

To fully understand the company, you'll want to know this set of people who are representative of the heart of Microsoft for a stretch of time when the company was small enough to feel like a crusade and a personal mission. We were the people in the middle, neither at the top nor the bottom of the food chain. We talk about where we came from, what our experiences were at Microsoft, and what we're doing now. Detail by detail, we paint a picture of our slice of Microsoft.

Everything changes over time, and the Microsoft I knew and loved is gone. It was such a wild ride and a great place to be that I wanted to put this book together to share what it was like. We've been written about many, many times by outsiders, but here, for the first time, we're telling our own stories.

I sent email asking people if they wanted to participate in this book, and I listed ten topics as a starting point. If you're interested in seeing the exact questions I sent, they're in the appendix. I wanted to give you a sense of how we came to be at Microsoft, what it was like for us, what we did, funny stories, observations about the company or the industry, and what we're doing now. Oh, and the money sometimes had a bit of impact on our lives.

Check the appendix for acronyms or terms that leave you baffled, such as "reorg," which you'll see a lot. It's short for reorganization, something Microsoft does constantly. Also, when you see the names Steve and Bill, that's Steve Ballmer and Bill Gates. Everyone was on a first-name basis and these two are the managers who really mattered and who were mentioned over and over. If you need more context for the stories, see the timeline in the appendix for a bit of the company's history and statistics.

Six women and thirteen men are included here, which doesn't match the actual ratio at Microsoft. As I recall, the ratio was usually something like 4:1 men to women. (An excellent ratio.) Eight of the people are developers, seven are in middle management, and four hold various other jobs.

Five are still working at Microsoft and the rest are either retired or well into their new careers, some of which are photographer, entrepreneur, musician, artist, rancher/mom, writer, helicopter pilot, and playwright.

Microsoft employees are often asked two questions: "Do you know Bill Gates?" and "Are you a millionaire?" There are a couple new Bill stories here and lots of mentions of Steve, but this book is not about the big guys. This book is about regular people who ended up in a company that went from nothing to worldwide recognition at warp speed and what our journey was like.

The chapters that follow are very different from each other in certain ways. Some are short, some are long, some are smooth narratives, others are a series of brief observations. They reflect the people whose lives they present: similar in their drive and energy, dissimilar in their particular viewpoints. Some chapters reveal a lot about the writers and their lives away from work, some reveal less, although if you read between the lines, the silence is significant. Some directly contradict others because people had different jobs, were in different groups, or were at the company during different years. Even so, some themes appear often.

We were part of a new phenomenon where stock option grants shared the corporate wealth with secretaries and people in the mailroom. We were part of a transition from the corporate nine-to-five mentality to the software industry's backbreaking culture where each employee was an entrepreneur, where those secretaries and people in the mailroom worked as hard at their jobs and took them as seriously as the bosses did theirs.

The personal computer barely existed when many of us joined the company, but there was something special about Microsoft. You had to be a little bit crazy to sign up with a company people didn't think would make it, in a business that no one's parents understood. You had to be a lot crazy about technology (or something) to stick with it when your personal life was swallowed up and you were making less money than you could somewhere else. We weren't a public company when many of us joined, and we were constantly fighting to survive, so we certainly didn't come to Microsoft for the big payoff. You can compare the experiences and motivations of early employees to those who joined later.

The puzzle of what kept people working like maniacs every day is in the chapters, too. Human resources departments everywhere claim to be looking for self-starting employees. Microsoft had that angle handled. We were a competitive bunch, self-starting because this was our arena, the world of ideas, where you were judged by your intelligence. Give professional athletes any kind of physical challenge, and they'll want to excel. Give Microsoft employees an intellectual challenge and watch them go.

I was struck by how many developers mentioned Steve Ballmer, who is now Microsoft's CEO. I hadn't realized how many people he hired or debriefed or motivated in some way. This guy was everywhere at once. He was Microsoft's secret weapon for years, although it's no longer a secret what kind of whirlwind force he is. He's even inspired a unit of measure: a *Ballmer* is how far Steve's voice carries through Microsoft's hallways, and it varies depending on whether his office door is open or closed.

Almost everyone's complaints are about things that got in the way of our doing the best job possible. Our focus was on doing good work and we hated being impeded in that. That speaks directly to the heart we put into our jobs. Nearly everyone mentions the caliber of his or her co-workers, mostly positively.

We all feel lucky that we got more than a salary at Microsoft, but from there the reactions are varied because the money has brought up different issues for each of us. You'll get a real-life glimpse into how people who came from working class or middle class families view life from the other side of the money gap. The dilemma of whether to tell people you're retired in your thirties turns out to be a tough one—it can create an insurmountable barrier with people you meet. And coming into sudden money reveals some of your true nature, which is not always a pretty picture.

All the people in this book are real; there are no composites and no apocryphal tales. The names of employees are fictitious except for co-workers who are public figures. The chapters aren't alike because people either wrote or dictated their own stories and their individual voices come through. You'll have a richer picture of the Microsoft experience by putting together these differing viewpoints, where we reveal Microsoft's flaws as well as our own.

I moved to Seattle with very little: clothes and a tiny old blue car with one orange door. That car dripped water on my leg when I made a right turn, and one day the hood started flapping as I drove down the freeway. I traded up to a car that had an electrical problem, and sometimes on dark back roads I suddenly found myself driving without lights. Banging on the dashboard seemed to help, or at least it made me feel like I was doing something. When I went job hunting, I had to puff up my résumé with every extra skill I could think of. I had one friend in Seattle.

Now my résumé and my life look very different. When I look in the mirror, I see a person shaped by Microsoft. And Microsoft was shaped by us.

Karin

It was so mind-bendingly weird to join a scrappy little company that grew up to be mighty Microsoft. It was just supposed to be a job! We rank-and-file non-techies have not attracted much media attention, so here's the first peek at what it was like. Later you'll hear from other liberal arts majors who also stumbled into Microsoft by dumb luck. Only in looking back do I see what a thin thread—one small choice after another—kept me on the path that led to fourteen years at Microsoft. The thought is unsettling, like the breathless feeling of narrowly avoiding an accident. I'm grateful for that thread.

For someone born in southern California, Seattle was too dreary and too far away to matter. Yet love has a way of changing the course of a life, and it did mine. I met a man in Seattle I thought I would marry, so I moved to Washington State, that drippy upper-left corner of the map, ready for my new life to begin.

As I applied for work, armed with my highly practical degree in French, I heard "Sorry, we're not hiring," over and over. When I asked who was hiring, a couple places mentioned Microsoft. I found the office and handed a résumé to the young woman at the front desk, which was the entire application procedure at the time.

A few weeks later I was invited to come interview. Rowland Hanson, the new Vice President of the marketing group, was looking for an Administrative Assistant. Although I made it into the final two, in the end he chose the other candidate. Rowland said that the International group might be a good fit for me and that he'd pass along my résumé. I thought this was the equivalent of "We'll keep your résumé on file" as it floated into the recycle bin, but Microsoft soon called again.

I survived the new round of interviews and learned I had won the coveted position of Administrative Assistant in the International group at a yearly salary of $15,000. I was also interviewing for a job at Paccar, a company that makes trucks, but it paid $50 a month less and didn't require any foreign languages. No contest. Although my offer letter from Microsoft didn't include the stock options the recruiter had talked a lot about, I happily took the job.

My dad likes to tell people about how he tried to persuade me that taking the job at Paccar would have been a good good idea—after all, those big trucks were darn exciting. Who knew how things would go for the unknown little software outfit I was also interviewing with? I didn't take his advice, he points out. And everyone laughs when he gets to the punch line: the name of that little software outfit.

All of 320 people worked at the company when I joined. Everyone went by their first name, even the managers at the top; there were no such perks as executive parking spaces, and you couldn't tell by dress, age, or manner who did what job.

We all worked long days, typically twelve hours or more. We were young, for one thing, and many of us were imported. We didn't have friends or family to turn to locally, so we hung out together. It reinforced our bond to Microsoft and kept the competitive juices flowing.

An admin's life is closely tied to the clock and the calendar and there is no way to fudge: either you got the shipment out on time, or it didn't go that day and you'd better be able to explain why not. My boss and I weren't very good at setting priorities and making the choices that entailed, so everything needed to be done right that minute. I literally ran through the halls between the mailroom, the front desk, and my office. I was 24 and he was 23, and no one was going to take the time to teach us how to work together effectively.

I became so frustrated with our situation that eventually I found an older manager—someone over thirty!—to talk to, and she helped me develop some tactics for communicating with my boss. Focus on the work, not the frustration. Ask him what his priorities are and make him choose what he wants first. It seems so simple now, but it worked and my boss and I got on track.

It was sometimes hard to block out the advice I was getting from friends and family. They didn't see the point in my putting in long hours, especially since overtime for salaried workers was unpaid, and I heard from various people how misguided I was to put up with it.

The unbelievable thing was that young people, often straight out of college, were thrown into real jobs. Real jobs with real consequences for not figuring things out: an order didn't get placed, a product didn't get finished on time. We had no training. There were no guidelines. There was no one to ask, there was nowhere to turn. Things changed so fast that even if someone knew the answers in January, by April the process or the people or the goal was different. Hierarchy? Minimal in those days, as we were all scrambling, everyone wearing multiple hats to get through the piles of work. If something needed to be done, and you were the closest warm body, you had to do it.

Assuming you could take that kind of pressure, this made it an excellent place to work. How else could you feel so proud of what you'd done? You knew you'd made something happen that couldn't have happened without you. There was really only one rule at Microsoft in those days: work smart.

Microsoft fought hard to enter a market and then to do well in it. We built the company piece by piece. I don't know why I say *we* like that, because I certainly had little to do with it. I was filing and answering the phone and typing personal letters for my boss and then later working on software manuals. I didn't make any of the deals or write code for the products that kept the company alive and growing madly, but this is part of working at Microsoft. It feels like *us* and *we* in a deep enough way that you are willing to choose the company over other parts of your life.

About six months after starting at Microsoft, I was sick of my job duties. Trouble was brewing at home, too. The man I'd moved to Seattle for was not the person I'd thought he was. I moved out, packing almost everything I owned into my little white Toyota, with my cat in her carrier perched on top of clothes and books. My personal life was about to get very interesting.

Microsoft didn't have a policy against dating within the company. Everyone did it, and there were no official repercussions. Things could get awkward within work groups, but that was an unofficial repercussion. Who else but a co-worker would truly understand that Friday nights, Sundays, or Christmas day were nice, quiet times in the office, perfect for getting more work done?

Two days after my move, a good-looking guy walked past my open office door. He stopped, came back, and started chatting, and a fun year with the handsome Yale grad began. When that ended, the jungle drums sent out the news. I broke up with the Yalie on a Saturday and the flood began on Monday. Guys were calling, guys were coming by my office, and guys were emailing me to ask me out. Never in my life had I experienced anything like this.

Suddenly my calendar was overflowing with dates, sometimes two in an evening, and usually six nights a week. These were very innocent: dinner and a movie, working out together, theater, parties. I had a strict kissing policy for these dates that meant no hand-holding, no good-night kiss, no nothing.

I grew up in a town small enough that many of us knew each other from grade school through high school. I was neither popular nor unpopular, but I was clearly branded Not Date Material and my fate was sealed until I left for college. College was good for my social life, but Microsoft was the mother lode.

Geeks are the nicest people. I mean your typical brilliant, often shy guy who was never popular, so he never had the chance to think of himself as God's gift to women. Yes, you had to overlook a certain amount of social awkwardness, which was somewhat difficult for a paragon of suave behavior like me. But these brainiacs were dying for attention and fascinating to talk to once they managed to get up the nerve to talk to a *girl*.

These were multifaceted, fun men. They skied and played soccer (some of them very badly, I will admit) and lifted weights and spoke German and did photography and read constantly. You single women who think there aren't any good guys out there: go for the smart ones.

Not surprisingly I ended up marrying someone I met at work. He was a nice, friendly guy, but not one of the geek boys I'd dated and enjoyed so much. Sadly, our marriage didn't last, although we gave it a good long try of nearly nine years.

✦

Fairly soon after I realized I hated being an admin, a job opportunity opened up that was a perfect fit for me. Microsoft had three foreign subsidiaries, in England, Germany and France, that were our toehold in having a global presence. There was a lot of pain to be gone through to make it a true presence, but it was a start. Now we needed products to sell in those markets. Okay, everybody, let's make some!

I became the first International Editorial Assistant. We created software user guides in foreign languages and soon my group was asked to do the first official desktop publishing project. It was my project and it went all right, considering that there was nobody to do the production work (the formatting of the text and the insertion of the pictures), no computer for that nonexistent body to use, and no space for that nonexistent computer being used by the nonexistent person.

One by one I dealt with these issues, making up the rules as I went, typical Microsoft protocol at the time. I "borrowed" a computer, found a freelancer, put her to work in a meeting room, and things kept moving along until the end of the project. Then my freelance formatter left, as scheduled, but the book was still not finished.

The younger brother of a Colombian employee happened to be visiting that week, so I ended up giving instructions in Spanish to Juan in the middle of the night while the two of us finished the project, the User's Guide for Italian Word. We'd work through the night and leave around eight or nine in the morning. I'd go home, sleep for a couple hours, eat lunch, and start working again. My parents happened to be visiting me that week, and I barely saw them. My hands shook all week from stress and fatigue, but we got the job done.

This was an important project for my group because it was the first in-house desktop publishing project and because Bill had personally promised the Italian subsidiary we'd hurry up and get them more products to sell. Months later, my boss mentioned that the Italian Word manual was sitting on a shelf because the software still wasn't done. I felt dizzy as the blood rushed out of my face.

It was a defining moment for me. I'd bashed my head against the wall for over two years, sacrificing anything to make my deadlines, and here, *once again*, due to shifting priorities and deadlines, it hadn't mattered. I decided that I would still work hard, and would do a lot for Microsoft, but I wasn't going to bleed for the company anymore.

So I pulled back my hours somewhat, and was rewarded for my job performance with a promotion. I was one of the luckier ones, though, that my job could be done more efficiently, that it wasn't a job that required marathon hours at the office. Not all jobs could be treated like mine; some were too visible or too critical to the future of the company.

The International group was the unwanted stepchild, a tiny market, at first, that had needs no other groups wanted to deal with. Other groups were working on their own impossible deadlines and didn't want to hear that a mailbox, complete with raised red flag showing there was mail to be picked up, would not be usable as an icon everywhere in the world. Shocking news: there were countries where things were different from the United States.

We were all learning together, and this globalization of products was quite complex. We don't usually spend much time thinking about how culturally biased we all are until we're forced to recognize other symbols, other languages, and other ways of thinking.

By 1985, my little documentation group had grown. The first Managing Editor was gone, done in by stress. The new manager was a gifted tap dancer, promising great things in meetings, then turning around and asking his small troupe to perform miracles. Being young and stubborn and ignorant and prideful, we did. Not too long after becoming a Production Editor, I was promoted to Managing Editor.

I'd now had three bosses at Microsoft, none of whom had ever managed anyone before. Now I was supposed to be a boss without ever having seen the job done well. I was 26 years old, in charge of six full-time people and up to 25 freelancers, at least one of whom was thirty years older than I was.

The first meetings I held were excruciating for me, as I was very shy in those early years. I'd prepare notes of what I was going to say. I hated having my slightly shaky voice be the only sound in the room, with everyone looking at me. I can still feel the closeness of those crowded meeting rooms, with all the chairs around the table filled and people standing against the walls, and me, just me, talking.

I'd get anxious about the pile of work I was responsible for: the long-range planning, the people management, the hiring (we interviewed almost a hundred people one summer), the scheduling, the process creation, the standard-setting, the training, the quality assurance, the space planning, the coordination with other groups, the *work*. Of course I was still expected to work as a Production Editor. And I expected it of myself. I realized, a few years later, that there was a little-known concept called "delegation" that some people used. Kind of handy when you couldn't clone yourself.

I began to understand what it was like to fight the same battles over and over, and to understand the difference between the enthusiastic new hires and the older employees who just wanted to come to work, put in their hours, and go home.

Part of the downside of having a company full of young people is that everyone still has a lot of rough edges. People haven't learned how to pace themselves, haven't learned diplomacy, and haven't learned the value of different work styles. A group needs the cautious, methodical people as well as the risk takers. It's hard to see, though, when you're the one who's burning with impatience to improve everything. It's a wonder we didn't drive our more experienced co-workers crazy. Or maybe we did, and they knew enough to keep quiet about it.

After three years in management, I grew frustrated with my situation. I was tired from years of learning everything the hard way, making mistakes, and doing it all at breakneck speed in a highly competitive environment. I was a decent manager, just inexperienced, and unable to live up to my perfectionist standard.

My parents were concerned that I was about to ruin my career when I told them I planned to step down from management, but things were different at Microsoft. Many of my programmer friends had tasted management and decided it wasn't for them without any negative consequences. I don't know whether that would be the case today, but back in the days when growth was so fast that just by hanging around you'd soon be the senior person in a group, you had quite a bit of individual power.

It felt like a free ride to keep my seniority and pay while doing fewer tasks, with no management responsibilities. It was a lot of fun to have the scales tip in my favor at last. I still worked hard and did what I was supposed to, but the pressure was off. I loved my new job doing training and quality assurance, a tiny subset of the work I'd been doing.

Then, after eight years in International working in foreign languages, I transferred to an editing job in the English-only Systems group. I came to see how critical it is to have a good manager. I had a manager with experience. One who trusted us and left us alone to do our work, and who fought for good raises, bonuses, and stock grants. His hands-off style had its drawbacks, the main one being that a couple people in our group should have had a little more scrutiny from above, but that was a small price to pay for having such a supportive manager.

One of Microsoft's strengths—and simultaneously one of its weaknesses—is the practice of pushing decision-making very low on the hierarchy. This means that individual managers can make decisions that affect their groups without running them by anyone. Freedom! Efficiency! And sometimes chaos!

There were also distinct pockets of culture within the company. I was used to having ten tasks, most of them urgent, waiting to be done. Now, on the domestic side of the company, there were periods of hard work, periods of normal work, and periods of no work at all. *No work*. We were "planning."

In reality, documentation is part of a product. If the programmers are stuck on what features are going to be included or are battling technical issues, you can't start the documentation. And editing builds in one more level of wait time, since you can't edit until the documentation is written. So sometimes the work down the line from the programmers stops. It's a shame that we couldn't admit that, but corporate politics dictated that we always act busy, usually "planning." I wish we could have been more real about it and gone and done something else during our down times.

Eventually my good boss moved to a new product team that was forming, and I decided to follow him. I spent my last few years at Microsoft back in management. Where years before my title had been Managing Editor, now I was riding off into the sunset as the Editing Manager. I wanted to get the bitter taste of management out of my mouth and see whether I could enjoy it. I found that I could the second time around.

✦

Here's something funny we do: we all have to mention how long we've been at Microsoft. Many letters to the company newsletter start out saying something like, "Having been an employee here for two years now," or "In the three years I've been at Microsoft," and the longer the tenure the better. You can play the game too. Are you a shareholder? Use that. "I've been an investor since 1986." Have you been reading about the company in newspapers or magazines? Go ahead and count it. "I've been following Microsoft for seven years now, and in my opinion…"

Don't you feel like an insider now?

✦

Microsoft from the inside is pretty different from Microsoft from the outside. The Microsoft I knew was tiny, carried along by lots of us, little ants running around as fast as we could, with huge stacks of work in our virtual in-boxes. From the outside, we looked like one big, smooth-running machine.

From the inside, you see the people. Regular people—okay, lots of super-smart regular people—making decisions and doing their jobs and carrying on in silly people ways. And I was always amazed at the number of people Microsoft found who would give up their lives for work. What was the secret?

When the company had a high percentage of programmers, their presence flavored the whole company. These geeks were in their element. This was even better than college because they could see their efforts going out into the world. The one thing these guys were loaded with, intelligence, was the one thing that counted.

People were constantly probing each other to see what they had. I was asked what my SAT scores were on a date; geek chitchat at its finest. Sometimes, watching guys try to determine who between them was smarter made me think of nature programs on TV where the male animals spar to see who's stronger.

I have perfected the social art of listening to techies discuss programming during parties, because early parties at Microsoft consisted of a room full of software developers rubbing their brains on their favorite topic. Imagine the excitement. There's a bowl of M&Ms, a bowl of chips, some beer, and a flock of geeks pontificating about APIs.

They talked about work constantly because they felt a real interest, a real passion, a real concern about whether our products were being done right. At first I would try to change the topic, but then I realized what was happening. Information, valuable information, was being exchanged. I kept my mouth shut and watched the information flow.

Those conversations could be scary. In fact, these guys were merciless in discussing the status of their projects. Nothing was good enough. All our products were on the verge of failing. They were all crap, but at least they were better crap than other companies were putting out.

I worried that we were about to lose our jobs, that Microsoft would be foundering any minute. But at these parties, engineers were letting off steam about projects that were driven too much by schedules and not enough by the joy of doing exactly the right thing. This non-work environment was also where they were free to criticize and maybe decide to bring up some of the points in a meeting or to just fix something if they could.

Maybe this is part of the puzzle of why Microsoft had so many dedicated employees. These guys loved the technology for its own sake, and for the chance to solve some difficult problems. They were attracted to the world of computing before it was everywhere: they came for the joy of the work itself, not for the sparkle of an industry with plentiful jobs and stock options. They were geek long before it was chic.

If you needed a company with good prospects and things like— gasp—benefits, you looked elsewhere. If you weren't interested in eating, sleeping, and breathing Microsoft, you looked elsewhere. If you weren't interested in constantly being challenged to jump higher and do it faster and now jump backwards and now upside down, you looked elsewhere. The bar was high, and everyone wanted to get over it. Well, not everyone, but most of those who weren't enthusiastic jumpers left the company fairly quickly.

The pressure was self-inflicted. If your boss wanted to force you on a death march you didn't want to participate in, you could quit. We were young, we had no mortgages, no families, no ties to anything. We could have walked away anytime. A few did, but most accepted undoable tasks as their personal challenges.

Something that I rarely saw at Microsoft was the person who said, "It's not in my job description." Most of us were willing to do just about anything. We didn't always do it happily, but we did it. We were very goal oriented, and we wanted to achieve what we set out to do, even when that meant rolling up our sleeves and doing several jobs at once.

Maybe another part of the answer is that many people, given this kind of incredible freedom and self-imposed challenge, will respond with their best effort. Or maybe it's that the tech industry generally hires people who've done well in school, an indicator of a willingness to simply *do the work*, whatever work it may be.

And it took a lot of hard work to turn things our way. For a very long time we were the little company no one had heard of. Now, Bill didn't call me into his office and explain his strategy to me, so I had a worm's eye view of the action. What I saw was fanatic dedication to technology. Not taking over the world, not getting rich, but solving problems that were really hard: *that* was considered worthwhile.

To be continued.

Roger

Gourmet cook, art collector, and physicist, he's just your average computer programmer. Roger has a compact build, dark hair, goatee, and brown eyes that don't miss a thing. His close-knit family and many friends clamor for invitations to his dinner parties. He's still slaving away at the 'Soft, whistling or singing as he goes about his day. Roger is an analytical guy with some funny stories about developers and insightful comments about how Microsoft and Apple were solving different problems. He also debunks some of the rumors that circulate about Microsoft.

When I joined the company in 1986, Microsoft was a public company, but we weren't in the public consciousness at all. In many cases, people didn't even know what programmers did.

There was a guy who had to convince his folks that he made lots of money to sit in front of a TV set. There was no touchstone with his parents' generation about programming—you couldn't compare it with anything they had known or done. I remember at one point my mom asked how I got those things to move on the screen. How do you program? I had to come up with a visual analogy for her.

No one came to Microsoft for the money in those days. They came because they simply wanted to code. There wasn't a lot of bureaucracy, there wasn't a lot of peripheral support staff or management up and down the chain. I think developers are still the same as they were before, but since there's a lower percentage of them now, their influence on the company's culture has been diluted.

Programmers can be weird puppies. One of the things Bill and Steve realized early on was the value of giving everyone their own offices: if you're interrupted all the time, you can't concentrate, and if you can't concentrate, you can't code. That privacy meant you could get away with certain things.

One weekend a developer I know was in his office, coding away. The recruiters, all women, used to work weekends too, and one of them knocked and then walked in without waiting for a response. When she started talking to the guy she suddenly realized that all he was wearing was a keyboard in his lap.

There was a guy who cashed out of Microsoft, put all his money in a backpack, and started traveling. When his backpack was stolen, he called Steve Ballmer collect and asked for his job back.

A guy I chatted with recently was telling me about how his grandmother sent him $25 for his birthday every year. Eventually he'd tried to tell her nicely that she didn't need to send him money, but she insisted, "You never know when you're going to need a little birthday present like that." After a while, he started automatically sending the money to charity.

A really smart guy, an intern who was arrogant and abrasive, came through one summer. Working with him, you'd think he had no compassion for other people. He then came back and worked full-time for Microsoft for a year or so before he left for something more fun. It was only then that we found out he'd sent half his paycheck home every two weeks to his mom, who was raising his sister alone.

A friend of mine has a very good sense of humor and is not afraid to use it. One year he made up a memo that he put into all the mailboxes belonging to summer interns. The memo said, "We're sorry, but we made a mistake and some of you should not have been hired. We're going to be administering tests to everybody and those who don't pass will be sent home. Part One is a programming test, and Part Two is a swimming test. We expect to see all of you at Lake Billg."

It was pretty clearly a bogus memo. This didn't stop plenty of interns from phoning their recruiters in a panic. Any intern who couldn't figure out it was a joke *should* have been sent home.

✦

It's interesting to hear the allegations about Microsoft and our deviousness. One of the best ones I heard was that we secretly moved all our resources from OS/2 to Windows in order to make Windows 3.0 and that we'd purposely misled IBM the whole time. In fact, the entire Win 3.0 team was hijacked to work on OS/2. There were maybe half a dozen people who eventually went *back* to Windows, but there was not a single person who went from OS/2 to Windows to help out with 3.0.

Then there was the claim that we had a saying: "DOS isn't done 'til Lotus doesn't run." This is stupid for two reasons. First, it was never, ever the case that we shipped something without all applications running on it. All apps run on our operating systems regardless of what company they are from. We had a list of applications to be compatible with, and we'd work our way down it, paying attention to every application out there. If people just look at the history of what we've done, they'll see the reality of it.

The second point is that if we were to ship an operating system that didn't work with other applications, people wouldn't buy it.

In the end, the customers decide what they're going to buy. If you piss off the customer, they'll decide not only to pass up that product, they'll decide not to buy any of our other products.

We were always accused of specifically setting out to break other companies' software when we released our operating systems, and that was fundamentally wrong. We *always* set out, one hundred percent of the time, to fix what we could fix, because that's what the customer wanted, pure and simple. We had to work around applications that had problems the creators weren't even aware of. In some cases you could not work around the problems. There's a lot of bad code in applications out in the world.

It's interesting to note that these accusations never went anywhere with the courts. There were a whole bunch of senseless, stupid allegations against us that were investigated by the FTC and found to be baseless. The DOJ found the same thing. Baseless.

✦

Apple has a huge benefit by having a closed hardware environment. You can't attach hardware from different manufacturers to your Apple computer, nor do you have multiple chip makers contributing to hardware. This matters because chips from various makers have weird little differences. Theoretically, different manufacturers make chips according to a rigid standard. The chips are supposed to be identical, but in reality they are not.

Our software has to compensate for those differences, but Apple doesn't have to deal with this issue. We've always had to do more work just to have the same level of functionality as Apple.

The benefit we brought to the PC environment was we truly hid a lot of the idiosyncrasies of the machines. The clone PCs were supposed to be identical to the IBM PC, but they weren't. We are required to have more developers to deal with the idiosyncrasies of the different brands of hardware, and to test all the different combinations of hardware and software.

So, first our operating system must compensate for differences between computers. Then, think of the many, many brands of all the different kinds of peripherals that can be attached to any of these PCs. The operating system has to understand them all. Not only does our operating system have to understand, say, a printer, it has to understand printers made by any manufacturer and any chip maker who has contributed to those printers. *Then* add all the software from other companies that we must be compatible with.

Every version of our Windows operating system had fewer and fewer bugs, but with every version of Windows, we found more problems because the number of combinations of hardware and software got bigger and bigger.

The problems we were encountering came out of the matrix of all the possible combinations of software (applications that could be running singly or simultaneously under Windows) and hardware (computers, video cards, printers, keyboards, mice, etc.). As the size of the matrix grew, it continued to expose the few remaining bugs. We ramped up the testing with each version because we had to, to respond to all these users and their configurations.

So you're trying to make everything work under Windows, and you have hardware with special considerations, and software programs from various manufacturers with their own hidden problems. It's a very, very complicated set of possible combinations.

An interesting thing happened when we shipped Win 3.0: we sold a million copies the first week. That kind of response was completely unprecedented, and it meant that we had a huge user base immediately trying to use Windows under all imaginable combinations of the matrix. People don't understand what an accomplishment it was when Windows 3.0 succeeded.

✦

There was no big money floating around when I came. Even people who'd been here since 1981 weren't rich, in spite of the IPO. Plus we were always thinking that we'd hit the top, that the stock couldn't get any higher. A bunch of people quit in 1988 saying that the stock was as high as it was ever going to go.

Microsoft has the most generous package in terms of rewarding employees. Hands down, Microsoft shares the wealth more than anyone else. It's a way of motivating and getting people. There weren't vulture capitalists [venture capitalists] involved, so Microsoft didn't give away the company right at the beginning. Bill and Steve and Paul [Allen] were willing to give stock to the employees. They were not cheap with us. They generated the wealth and then shared it, which created the Puget Sound economy we have today.

Some people chose not to come here because they were sure Microsoft wasn't going to make it. One of my housemates at Princeton who was getting a Ph.D. in Computer Science came out to interview, got a job offer from Steve, and didn't accept it because he thought we didn't have any future.

Emily

Emily takes us deep into her head and her heart. We don't hear about her day-to-day activities; instead we hear about how Microsoft built her up, showed her the sky, and then let her fall. She's a sturdy Midwestern woman, blonde and blue-eyed, with the thick glasses of the perpetual reader. She's a deeply loyal friend, a woman who travels, has season tickets to the opera, the symphony, and the Mariners. She describes the first time she exercised stock options. "I remember staring at all those zeros. I'd been very methodical and detached until that moment. Suddenly, my heart started pounding. I was shaking."

I was as happy at Microsoft as I could be and I was as unhappy as I could be. Sometimes on the same day.

I'm most happy when I'm part of a group—not necessarily a cohesive or uniform group, but a loose affiliation. Microsoft was like that. You were part of a big, dysfunctional family. We all spoke the same language. We had the same shorthand. We told the same jokes, with the same punch lines. We had the jargon. We had the history, we shared the trials and tribulations and triumphs. We had the same enemies.

When I first got to MS, I laughed about the people who let Microsoft become their whole life. If you had any gaps in your life, MS would fill them. You didn't need to buy clothes cuz you had a steady stream of product T-shirts to wear. No social life? No problem, there were the Microtones if you liked to sing, or the soccer teams, or the single parents group, or the gay and lesbian group. Or the easiest thing of all: just bury yourself in the work. You get home around 8 p.m., warm up something in the microwave, stare at the TV for a while, go to bed, get up, guzzle coffee, and go back to work.

Unlike a lot of others, I'd had the advantage of having worked at other jobs before coming to MS, so this gave me a bit of perspective. I'd already worked 60-hour weeks during crunch times. I had already pushed myself to go into work when I was sick as a dog. I had already forfeited unused vacation time because there was no way to get away from work. So in many ways, Microsoft's high-pressure work environment was not new for me.

What was new was the fun, the loopiness, the sense of family, the warmth. I was charmed by the guys wearing garbage can lids while jousting with broom handles. Unicyclists patrolled the parking lots, and shirtless guys pranced on the basketball court for their mid-afternoon break. I never attended any of the Friday afternoon parties that broke out spontaneously every week, but I marveled at them. I was impressed that they'd built this beautiful little campus around the ravine, stream, and trees instead of plowing them under and paving them over. I'd always hated dressing up for work. People here wore Bermuda shorts and tank tops. Their offices looked like dorm rooms, complete with pyramids of pop cans. Email circulated a warning to be careful in the Building 5 parking lot; a mama duck was parading her ducklings around. I felt so at home.

What was new was the opulence. At the job I had before Microsoft, you had to ask the office manager for a Post-It notepad. One. She would open a desk drawer, take out a key, use it to open another drawer, reach inside and carefully take out one single Post-It notepad, and hand it to you gravely. You knew you'd better not ask for another any time soon. At Microsoft, each building had four supply rooms stacked with Post-It notepads, floppy disks, pens, pads of paper, letterhead, file folders, labels of all colors, you name it. Nobody stood guard. The kitchens had every conceivable beverage, free. Even Clamato. There was powdered soup in the cupboards for those long nights after the cafeterias were closed. Each building had a patio area outside where we'd eat at the umbrella-covered tables during nice weather.

What was new was the infectious exhilaration of doing something unique, something new and exciting and cool. It was impossible to miss the buzz: the enthusiasm, the passion, and the excitement. The first company meeting I attended, one product team wore the same product T-shirts and sat together so they formed a big yellow block in the crowd. They ranted and screamed like banshees. They really meant it. As time went on and Microsoft became better known, the IBM jokes, the Apple slurs, the Novell and Lotus insults all became meaningful and relevant. As I personally became more committed to the work we were doing, I found myself defending the company when "outside" people told Bill Gates jokes.

I maintained emotional detachment for a while, but eventually they broke me down. I was seduced. I fell in love.

It was like being picked first when splitting into teams in Phys. Ed. class. You couldn't help feeling a little flattered that they wanted you. Later on, it was like being in a cult. You lost your individuality when you became a Microsoftie. You started to see the world only as it related to Microsoft.

For a long time, Microsoft amply fed my need to be a Microsoftie but it was a dysfunctional relationship. There were times when it was abusive. It wasn't enough to just show up and work hard, oh no. You had to open your heart and mind and give your whole self to the work. You were only as good as your last performance evaluation. You had to merge with the collective. Resistance was futile.

But as time went on, things started to change. My first work group in International was a model of unity and clarity in many ways. We had common goals and we all worked towards them. We had been told to cooperate and work together, and we obeyed. Later on, certain upper-level managers at MS believed we would do better work with a competitive relationship between groups. Teamwork only went so far; then the other groups became *them* and not *us*.

Withholding vital information like true schedule milestones became the default for a variety of reasons. Upstream in development, there was always conflict between what was desired (published) and what was achievable (real). Those of us downstream were victims of that disconnect—with budgets, product schedules, extra staffing, and external vendors all hinged on schedules we *knew* were bogus. We learned how to interpret the misinformation and cultivated sources in upstream work groups to help us predict our work load. This quickly became outrageously stupid. To my knowledge, that's how it's done today.

From time to time, a new hotshot would come into your orbit and decide to remake your group in his image. And that team you so lovingly created would simply disappear. Reorged. This sounds simple enough, but over time, I began to see it as an exotic form of mental torture. One day you are earnestly devoting yourself to the goals of the group, which are of the utmost importance. You have timelines and deadlines and budgets and staffing forecasts and training plans. And then there's a meeting. And all of a sudden, not only are your projects no longer important, your little group isn't important anymore either. There is now a new Big Picture, a new Strategic Plan, a world where you're running on old news. The guillotine drops.

The first couple of times this happened, it was devastating. The disbelief, fear, and outrage were so tangible, it vibrated off the walls. People had always said these things didn't happen at Microsoft: we weren't like Boeing or Safeco or those other horrible big corporations. One co-worker was assigned to report to a hated ex-manager; she compared it to a battered wife being forced to return to her abusive husband.

After a while, the reorgs were not a surprise, but were no less destructive and disruptive. One of the worst things I've ever had to do was lay off good people for no real reason. "Reductions in force" became commonplace across the country in the early and mid nineties, but for many of us at Microsoft it felt like betrayal. As middle managers, we sucked it up and did our best to cope with the fallout. Focus on the tasks at hand. Calm peoples' fears. Reassure. Make an agenda for the next meeting, set up a timeline. Claw the knife blade out of the middle of your back. And try to numb your own grief and anger. It was pulverizing.

Then, through a series of unfortunate circumstances, I found myself reporting to the most appallingly bad manager I'd ever had. I simply was not able to disguise my contempt for this person. He spent a year cajoling me, complimenting me, trying to enlist me as an ally. The more he tried, the more I hated him. Finally he gave up and started reassigning my responsibilities to others. I had to watch less qualified people screw up projects I knew like the back of my hand. Meanwhile, I spent a lot of time playing Taipei waiting for my new assignments, which never came.

These had been important projects I was committed to, projects I cared about, some I'd worked on for years. His bad management resulted in disastrous failures, both near-term and long-term. I knew that soon he would get a black name around the company; guilt-by-association is very powerful at Microsoft. I wanted nothing to do with anything he did.

I spoke to the appropriate people about my concerns. I went through channels. For reasons I'll never understand, the management above him decided to back him. I had always believed in the essential good sense of the management at Microsoft. I know they must have had their reasons. But at that point, I lost all faith in them.

I spent six months looking for another job within the company. But for someone with my skill set and experience, I had already done everything there was to do. Even Microsoft has its limitations.

After nearly eight years at the company, I was one of the old-timers. I started feeling like a dinosaur. Higher-ups would point to me and talk about the valuable wealth of knowledge and experience I brought to the group, but nobody wanted to put it to work.

Then one of my friends advised me to update my financial spreadsheets, saying I probably had more money than I thought. I did so and to my shock and amazement, I had more than enough money to walk away. Still, it took me another six months to leave. Part of it was the disbelief about the money. But a big part of it was accepting the fact that it was time to go.

I've never really gotten over Microsoft. I can talk about the experience with MS friends, in particular with people who were there at the time. But I have rarely discussed it with non-Microsofties. It hurts too much, even now. It was like having your heart broken by the love of your life. It still hurts. Maybe you never really get over it.

I loved Microsoft because for the first and only time in my life someone let go of the reins and gave me my head. Someone said, "Take your best shot, give it all you've got," and I did, and I succeeded, and I was rewarded.

I loved Microsoft because I was surrounded by people I liked and admired. Even the ones I didn't like, I had to admire. They were well educated, talented, bright, passionate, articulate, energetic, and usually very good at what they did. Most important, they weren't content with "good enough."

I loved Microsoft because, yes, it was full of geeky programmers. It was fun living in a world where the skinny guys with thick glasses ruled the roost. My brothers were geeks, and so were their friends, and so were some of my best friends. I like their world.

I loved Microsoft because the others who worked there were interesting, multidimensional people from all walks of life: poets, painters, teachers, travel agents, architects, car salesmen, singers, philosophy majors. People who worked at print shops or for neighborhood weeklies. People who danced ballet, who delivered pizza, who spoke Rumanian. At the time I started, most of the non-development staff had been pulled from the non-tech world, since software was a new industry. People who were cooks for logging crews, who sang Bulgarian folk music. They were eclectic, funny, and full of energy. They thought creatively. They took risks. They were endlessly fun and interesting to be around, and they inspired me.

I loved Microsoft because it was my family. They have seen you at your best and your worst. They know all your flaws. They have the same scars. They know why you do what you do without having to ask. They drive you crazy sometimes. But they understand.

I loved Microsoft because I was surrounded by the best. Everything was topnotch, five-star. For the first time in my life, I was enveloped in abundance, and it felt really good.

I loved Microsoft because it was always balls to the wall with everything. All my life people have been telling me to tone it down. *Nobody* toned it down at Microsoft.

When people tell me something about Microsoft now, I don't really want to hear it. The Microsoft that I loved is in the past. The giant corporation out there in Redmond today has very little to do with the spunky, fun company I worked for. There is no point missing something that doesn't exist anymore.

Nonetheless, I hold MS up as a standard by which to judge all other endeavors. That experience was unequalled in terms of quality of people, quality of work, and quality of fun. It proved to me that it was possible to work very, very hard, do excellent work, and have fun doing it.

When I was getting ready to quit Microsoft, I wrote a long letter to my grandparents. I went into some detail about stock options: how I got them, how they worked, and why I had so much money. I didn't give exact amounts, but I told them that if I lived modestly and if the stock market stayed stable, I would not need to work anymore. I explained that I was telling them this because I didn't want them to worry when they heard that I'd quit my job.

My grandfather, as was his habit with important documents, dated the bottom of it. We found it amongst his papers after he died. They did not reply; none was called for.

My family ignores my money. I'm from the Midwest; we are creatures of moderation and harmony. We avoid controversy. When we're confronted with something out of the ordinary and are required to comment, we remark quietly, "Well, that's different." I have not given money to my family. It's not because I'm stingy or mean. It's not because I don't love my family. It's because money changes things; once you give someone money, it changes the terms of your relationship.

It's also because sometimes giving someone money is the last thing they really need.

My non-Microsoft friends don't ask about the money either. They might raise an eyebrow at some of the things I do, like flying to Los Angeles to see an art exhibit or to Phoenix for Mariners spring training. But anyone who knows me well knows I am a creature of passions. I don't like opera—I *love* it. You may say well, sure, she has time to do that, but I was like this before I had money. Having money just makes it easier.

That passionate nature and intensity of focus may be part of what helped me survive and indeed thrive at Microsoft. It was a place for intense people. And that in turn led to the stock options.

Okay. How did I end up with all that money?

I earned it.

I was lucky.

I was smart.

Yes, I earned it. During my time at Microsoft, stock options were granted once a year to selected individuals as a special reward for contributions above and beyond the call of duty. I can honestly say that I earned them and I deserved them, based on my performance in comparison with those around me. I worked my ass off and gave everything I had every day. But more importantly, I got results. It wasn't just a matter of working hard. I consistently *exceeded* the objectives set for me. Microsoft got its money's worth from me.

On the other hand, I was lucky. I was lucky I got pointed their direction in the first place. I was lucky I had the skills they needed. I was lucky I got hired. I was lucky I had managers who promoted me and acknowledged my work with stock grants. I was lucky I worked in teams with other people just as committed and just as determined to succeed.

On the *other* other hand, I was smart about the money. We all know lots of people who squandered their stock options on bad choices. I didn't cash them out to buy a car as soon as I vested. I ignored them. During the years I ignored the options, the stock split and split and split. I never bothered to keep track of how much the options were worth. Ignoring them was the best possible strategy for getting rich. Okay, okay, I admit it. What I just told you was more about ignorance, laziness, and luck than making smart choices. But nonetheless, I did not cash out and spend the money as I vested, and that's the point. A lot of people did.

It was a very weird, surreal thing to be 37 and retired. It separates you from other people. In the months after I quit my job, I found myself at large during daylight hours on weekdays: me, the full-time moms with their toddlers, and the normal gray-haired retired people. I felt like they were looking at me. Why aren't you at work?

✦

Every day I wake up and ask myself: how in the hell did I get so lucky? I wonder about it while sitting at stoplights. I mull it over while I brush my teeth. My Microsoft friends and I band together and huddle over our lattés, like a little encounter group: it's okay to have this money, honest.

I don't know what I'd do if I didn't have my MS friends to talk to. It's nice to have money, but it doesn't erase pain or fill up the empty places. It doesn't make a sick child well. It doesn't stop parents from dying. It doesn't keep your wife from lying or your husband from drinking. Sometimes you feel like you don't deserve to consider anything a problem because you're so lucky. My MS friends know that's bullshit. Thank God for them.

✦

For the most part, I live a very ordinary life; there is little outward evidence of my money. My neighbors would have no way of knowing. This is the outward evidence of my money:

The fact that I don't work.

My season tickets to the opera (box seats, no less).

My frequent travel to Europe.

A small waterfront cabin in the San Juan Islands north of Seattle.

I have my little luxuries. I hire someone to clean my house, and I hire someone to do my yard work. But so do a lot of "normal" people around here.

One of the genuine pleasures of having this money is giving presents. I really enjoy being able to be generous with gifts without a second thought. I don't do it often, though, because people can start to resent it. You have to be sensitive to that.

On the other hand, I wear well-worn Levis. The Gap sweatshirts crowding my closet are 10 years old. My car is 12 years old. My house is comfortable but modest. I don't have DSL or cable modem. I am easily amused.

✦

There was one moment when the enormity of the fact of the money hit me like a brick: the first time I exercised stock options. The money was to pay off the mortgage on the house, amounting to around $110,000. Mind you, at that time, I had never handled more than a few thousand dollars at one time in my life, maybe a car loan or something.

I remember sitting at my desk getting the confirmation of the transaction. I remember staring at all those zeros. I'd been very methodical and detached until that moment. Suddenly, my heart started pounding. I was shaking. I couldn't sit still. I stalked back and forth in my office, muttering, "Oh my God, oh my God." I went outside and stood at the back door smoking cigarette after cigarette with trembling hands. I went back inside and called a girlfriend and screeched to her in a high-pitched whisper.

I was quietly losing it. I finally just had to go home. It took hours to quiet the breathless, vibrating feeling. I still have little fluttery moments from time to time, but nothing like that.

✦

After Microsoft, many of us get involved in volunteer work or the nonprofit world, which is a rude shock. We aren't used to counting pennies. The nit-picking, counterproductive administrative bullshit at most nonprofits is enough to drive many of us away.

The travel people do is fascinating. I just got a post card from Antarctica.

My female friends with children want to make up for lost time and throw themselves headlong into full-time motherhood. Many of them apply the same energy, time, and imagination to parenting that they once spent at Microsoft. They are on the ball, knowledgeable, well read, and tireless.

For a few years, it's rewarding, but like all human creatures, they need more. Some of them become one-dimensional and brittle. Some become depressed and isolated. Some of them reconnect with friends and/or find their way into other activities once the kids are in school.

The men tend to play with toys or have excellent adventures. They buy things and go places. They're more likely to make a business of their hobbies. One guy flies to Europe to play golf once a year. One guy is in trouble with gambling and has lost his job, wife, and daughter. Some guys continue working to enable the wives to stay home with the kids and live in a really expensive house with a really expensive lifestyle.

There's an unfortunate pattern: get all this money, create your dream house, wreck your marriage, sell the dream house. If I were a divorce lawyer, I'd watch the Building Permits section in the Legal Notices part of the newspaper.

Some people get more politically conservative. Sometimes having money can make you want to hang onto it tighter. You resent anyone trying to take your hard-earned money away from you, even though those few tax dollars amount to less than what you spent on a pair of shoes. You can fall into the self-righteous hole and figure *I got mine, let them get theirs.* I've seen that happen more than once. But thankfully, that seems to be the exception. Having money can allow you to tap into an inner generosity too. Many people give away a lot of money. They devote themselves to service and good deeds. The Puget Sound area is awash in Microsoft money and volunteer workers. It's a good thing.

You can get lost without an anchor in your life. Work provides so much more than just a paycheck. Being needed, feeling you have something worthwhile to contribute, taking pride in what you do. Being part of a community, a family. The need to learn, to improve, to better yourself. The satisfaction of achieving a goal, of completing a task or beating a deadline. Right or wrong, we base much of our identity on what we do.

Not working can be very isolating. Without that daily structure of a job, some drift off and fall prey to life's hazards. I'm not talking about drugs or alcohol as much as loneliness, disconnectedness. Trying to buy happiness. Forming odd attachments. Losing your sense of self. Depression. Drifting, aimless lives are a nice vacation, but you don't want to live there full-time.

Eventually, many people get some kind of job again, part-time or temp. They go into business for themselves, or they create a job out of volunteer work. Many devise a schedule of job-like activities that structure their lives. We seem to need to work.

✦

People's attitudes, if you tell them you have money, are uniformly predictable. *Gee, must be nice.* They get a faraway look in their eyes. *I know what I'd do if I didn't have to work.* You may as well hand them the rose-colored glasses. They don't listen to your answer because of the visions dancing in their heads. They *need* to see it as a utopia, a nirvana. *All life's problems can be solved by money.* If I didn't have to work, I could be a better mom. Our marriage would be fine if we didn't have to fight about money all the time.

They won't hear you when you tell them otherwise, so you stop trying. You're no longer a real person to them. They don't hear you, they don't see you. This is the single biggest issue for in my life after Microsoft. It helped destroy my marriage: my husband stopped listening to me and stopped seeing me.

Money changes everything, and it changes nothing. It's like love. Not having it can surely make you miserable, but having it is no guarantee of happiness. In the long run, you create or destroy your own happiness. Money is a tool, you use it however you choose. I am no more or less happy now than I was when I was poor.

Yeah, I'm less stressed out. Life is more comfortable and relaxed. I can travel to places I've dreamed of seeing. I can rent a car when I visit relatives instead of mooching rides. I can fix all those little broken things around the house. I can go to all the movies I want. I can buy books and CDs to my heart's content. I can socialize with friends.

I'm lucky and I know it, and I'm grateful for the good in my life.

Stewart

Stewart is one of those gifted people, talented at everything he does. Computer programmer, martial artist, writer, world-traveling guy with a huge circle of friends. He's on everyone's invite list. He cut his shoulder-length wavy hair a few years ago, but still wears a beard and glasses. He has a beautiful young wife and baby daughter. He explains what it's like to program, the engineer's search for perfection, and tells funny stories of working in the foreign culture of IBM.

When I became a computer programmer, my family had no idea what I was doing. My mother was quite skeptical of the whole enterprise, preferring that I become a doctor, or failing that, a lawyer, or titled nobility: anything with some social cachet. Computer programming was a trade, not a profession. My father had used computers when he was a professor in business school, but he was long dead when I went to college.

My mother's attitude was illustrated when she asked me how my computer science degree from Yale differed from ads she saw in the back of matchbooks that said, "Become a computer programmer in seven months!" Not having taken the correspondence course, I couldn't say.

A number of my friends from college went to work at Microsoft before I graduated. They convinced me to go to an on-campus interview with a former Yale graduate student we'll call Don. This was maybe my second or third formal interview for a real job, so I was scared and unsure of what to do. Don proceeded to grill me on the gossip in the Computer Science department—who was sleeping with whom, for how long, was the situation stable, etc.

At the time I was living with a computer science grad student who had superhuman powers of social perception, so I aced the interview. Don decided that I was the sort of person they needed at Microsoft. In retrospect, I now presume they were hiring me to be a gossip columnist for Slate's launch more than a decade later. I was another example of Microsoft's famed long-term strategy.

I was flown to Seattle, where I underwent what at the time was the typical Microsoft interview process, a set of five to six one-hour interviews, extemporaneously solving technical problems on a whiteboard. They made me an offer at the end of the day for a summer internship.

I moved to Capitol Hill in Seattle, a very hip neighborhood filled with men who love men, women who love women, artists who love themselves, and punks who love no one. I didn't fall into any of those categories, but had a good time anyway.

The second day I showed up at work, I couldn't get in my office— the door gave a little in a bouncy way, but wouldn't open. I looked through the hole in the door where there'd been a lock, and all I could see was pink. I forced the door open a crack to find that my office was completely filled with a huge pink weather balloon. My managers had decided I was someone with a sense of humor, and I decided I really liked the Microsoft culture.

Another thing that convinced me to come back to the company full-time the next summer was the challenging work. I was in the Xenix group, which produced a licensed version of Bell Lab's UNIX. My job, which I found incredible for a college student, was profiling the Xenix kernel to find out how it spent its time and what it was doing, then rewriting the disk head travel routines to try to improve the speed of disk access.

This was hog heaven. I had just had an operating systems class the semester before, and here I was at a real company doing work that might go out in the real world. I learned an enormous amount about programming in those three months, just from the pace and the intellectual freedom.

In earlier days, there was an informal policy that summer hires were not given work that would ship with the product because they disappeared back to their universities and couldn't fix bugs that were found later, or upgrade the code for future releases. And often summer interns were not ready to do work that would ship. So I was doing mostly testing and research. It was more fun than writing product code turned out to be, because I didn't have such tight deadlines. In later years, as the programmer crunch became tighter at Microsoft, summer hires were put to work on shipping product code, which I felt was a mistake.

✦

Programming is hard. It may not be as hard as pure math or theoretical physics, but it's a very intellectually challenging activity. It's not like other kinds of engineering. It may not even be engineering in the strictest sense of word, but a hybrid of art and engineering. Certainly getting code fast and bug free is extremely difficult in a large system.

One of the things I liked at Microsoft was that most of the programmers there, in addition to being very bright, cared about writing quality, robust code. There are notable exceptions and I won't name them because I signed a piece of paper saying I wasn't going to say anything libelous, but you know who you are.

People cared about their code being as bug free as possible and were willing to sacrifice their weekends and social lives in order to write the best code they could. It was an attitude I saw throughout my twelve and a half years at Microsoft. Were I to have had a social life, I would have happily sacrificed it. Luckily, I never had to make that choice. The engineers' commitment to quality never diminished with the increasing size of the company.

Many engineers felt that management would compromise quality because, rightly or wrongly, engineers like to over-engineer things, and management likes to ship things. A healthy tension between these can produce good products and a good bottom line. That tension also creates a stereotypical dynamic, though: engineers want more time for the product because they could work out a few more bugs or add a few more features. Managers say no, we need to ship. Junior members of both sides portray the other side as satanically misguided.

"Management/marketing is forcing me to ship this product! I've only worked on it for five years and it's not done yet. It still has bugs in it. If they'd only give me another year, it would be perfect."

"The developers want to destabilize the whole product to fix this one bug where the dialog box comes up with the colon truncated from the button text if you're searching for a text string longer than 512 characters. What is wrong with them?"

I think the product that most suffered from this was Word for Windows, which went through five million incarnations and took something absolutely ridiculous like six years to ship in an industry with a one- to two-year product cycle. But it was going to be perfect. In fact, they'd never have to revise it once it shipped.

Even when we were a very small company, before Microsoft ruled the world, stalking like Tyrannosaurus Rex, we were aware of the perceptions of arrogance. I coined a phrase for our reputation, "Not arrogant, merely correct," which I felt summed up a great deal of Microsoft's internal thinking: it's not arrogance if you're right. This was said with tongue in cheek, but as it spread through the company, people took it more seriously than I had intended.

Computer programmers are often arrogant. They feel they are brighter than everybody else, which may or may not be true, and that they are the high priests of the machine and nobody else understands what they do. For programmers, coding rules both their status within the company (independent of the corporate hierarchy) and also rules their thoughts, because it's a tremendously engaging and engrossing activity.

Good code has an elegance to it, somewhat akin to the elegance of a good mathematical proof. Elegance is doing something in a minimal amount of time in a way that is both clear and simple. It's doing something in such a way that anyone can understand what it does, can modify it, and can extend it to do other things.

Programmers are optimists at work, regardless of their outlook on the rest of life. You have to be an optimist because when you write a program, you undertake a few steps: you write the code, then you compile it (which means translating it from an English-like language like C or Pascal, into something the computer understands, the binary representation). After you compile the code, you run it to see how it works. Each of these steps is an opportunity for you to discover errors you have made.

When you compile code, the compiler (which is another program) reads your code and says okay, if X is greater than 3, he wants to turn the screen blue, and if X is less than 3 he wants to check Y, and if Y is greater than 2 he wants to turn the screen pink, and if Y is less than 2 he wants to turn the screen black—the program may follow any of these little logical paths. In any one of these, if you've forgotten a semicolon or a comma or a period, the compiler will emit a large warning and tell you that on line 167 you have a syntax error. Compilers are like your worst nightmare of high school English teachers: any mistake, any slang, any misplaced punctuation, any lack of subject-verb agreement will cause the compiler to spew hundreds of warnings.

Programmers are optimists because they always hope that the next compilation and test will work perfectly, even though experience has shown that there will always be another error previously obscured by the last error. So each compilation and test run is an act of faith. Theoretically you can program as fast as you can type and most programmers type very fast. The only thing slowing you down is your own stupidity. In theory, if you were perfectly smart, you'd just type the program, compile it, run it, and you would be done.

So why does it take us six months to write ten thousand lines of code we could type in a week? The answer is we make lots of mistakes. Thousands of them. We go down blind alleys, we try things and then have to back out of them. The programs we write are so large, we can't hold them in our heads all at once. We have to write them in small pieces, and then we realize the pieces don't quite fit together.

Programming *should* be enormously humbling. Unfortunately, most programmers don't seem to think this way, and they believe the fact that they get it wrong slightly less often than other people is grounds enough for the arrogance. I suppose if programmers were realists, they would be paralyzed by the evidence of their incompetence and no one would write software.

✦

Microsoft did an extremely good job at managing the esprit de corps and keeping the work environment reasonable even as the company grew. There were changes, but the amount of administrivia and bureaucratic nonsense was incredibly low compared with the other companies I had seen or worked with.

When I was with Microsoft Consulting Services, I worked with the computing or IT departments of many other organizations: airlines, banks, telephone companies, government departments, some extraordinarily paranoid defense ministries, etc. So I had a little taste of life among our customers, albeit in Australia.

Every time I left a company and went back to Microsoft, I breathed a sigh of relief and said, "I am so glad I work for a company that doesn't actually care when I get to work, what I wear, what I eat, with whom I sleep, or how I spend my free time." As one high-ranking software architect told me early in my career, "I don't care if you have sex with sheep in your office as long as the code runs on time." That's an attitude that I really appreciated. Not that I had a thing for sheep, or ever had sex in my office with anything or anyone, but it was comforting to think that I could, if anything or anyone ever wanted to have sex with me. Provided I was on schedule, of course.

✦

One of my mid-career experiences was liaison duty with IBM, at their division in Boca Raton, Florida. At that time, IBM was the huge juggernaut, profit machine, owner of the computer industry, and grand behemoth that it no longer is today.

I was put in a little office suite rented by Microsoft and we were told that we would help fix this product that the two companies were developing. It was called OS/2; it was an operating system that didn't go very far. My previous project had been cancelled so I was demoralized and unhappy, and now I'd been told that I was going to be shipped away from my life for six weeks to live in this air-conditioned hellhole.

It was incredible to see what IBM was like compared to Microsoft. They had casual Fridays where you could wear slacks and an open-collared shirt; they had vending machines so that if you wanted a cup of coffee with artificial creamer you had to find 35 cents. They had little card keys and you couldn't tailgate through the door. Everybody had to swipe their card key, go through the door, and then close the door in the face of the person behind them, with whom they'd just eaten lunch. IBM tallied security violations, so if you were caught tailgating through the secured door too many times, you'd be fired.

Microsoft engineers racked up more security violations per day than an IBM employee could have in a year because we didn't follow the dress code and we didn't care about tailgating through the door.

We left things on our desks that were proprietary, confidential papers. We felt that the IBM security guards stalking the building at all hours would probably protect our little papers saying that we'd like the Escape key to make the dialog box disappear, and that even if this leaked out to the world press, it might not upset the global balance of power.

There were a couple experiences I had with IBM that I really enjoyed. The first was that my office was much too cold; it had that typical Floridian air-conditioning-to-the-point-of-freezing, and I would freeze in my casual Monday–Friday business-wear shorts. Business-wear was a code word at Microsoft for clothing with hemmed cuffs.

I called up the maintenance people and said, "My office is much, much too cold. Could you turn the air conditioning down?"

They said, "We need a manager's authorization to adjust the temperature in your office."

"Well, you know, I hate to sound like a complainer, but I'm actually able to determine whether I'm too cold without my manager. He's 3,000 miles from here, in Redmond. He might be too warm, for all I know. I'm here by myself on liaison duty, I'm not IBM staff."

"You need to get an IBM manager to sign off on changing the temperature in your office."

"I don't know any IBM managers. They only let me talk to the programmers here."

"You need an IBM manager's authorization to adjust the thermostat."

"Okay, no need to adjust the thermostat. I'm going to buy some epoxy and a dinner plate, and glue the plate over the air vent. Then the air conditioning will just leak in under the door and I'll be warm enough."

"You're going to glue a dinner plate over our HVAC vent?"

"Sure. Send me back to Seattle."

"You know, *my* manager would sign off on making your office warmer. That would be perfectly fine."

"Great, that's wonderful. Thanks."

The second encounter involved my decision to use the Tab key to move between data entry fields when you typed in a dialog box. IBM said, "Oh, no, we need to have a meeting on this."

So they held a meeting and escalated the decision up two levels of management, where the people said to me, "No, no, we don't think the Tab key is the right key; it should be some other key."

"I still think it should be the Tab key."

"Well, we'd like to escalate it to your manager."

"Sure, go ahead."

And my manager said, "Yeah, whatever Stewart says, he's a smart guy. Just do what he says—he's there, he's the engineer, that's why we pay him."

IBM escalated it another two levels in their organization, and eventually it got to a Vice President who agreed, "We don't think it should be the Tab key."

My manager said, "Yeah, okay, I looked at it and Stewart is right, so Microsoft thinks it should be the Tab key."

"Listen, we've escalated this four levels up our management chain, and we're still just talking to a second-level manager at Microsoft? We want to go up four levels in your management chain so we have equality in this negotiation."

"I don't think BillG's mother is *interested* in this. I'll ask my manager about it, I'll ask whether he trusts Stewart on the Tab key, and he'll say yeah, and we'll go back to where we are now, but I am not going to bother anyone else with what the Tab key should do in a dialog box."

Microsoft provided a strong sense of identity for many of the programmers there, particularly as it became successful. It provided a mark of intellectual status: you were doing work that had cool worldwide implications. So there was status in technical circles associated with being a Microsoft programmer.

Social life at Microsoft centered around Microsoft. We developers tended to live together in large geek clusters, or as one young woman of my acquaintance said at her first Microsoft party, "Wow, geeks come in herds!" During my first summer, I dated one of the few female programmers. When I returned as a full-timer, I didn't date anyone from work, but my social life was rich in friendships. We were a tightly knit team; we went to lunch together every day, and we often ended the day by going out to dinner and a movie.

People lived in a dawn-to-dusk Microsoft environment: Microsoft roommates, Microsoft friends, Microsoft co-workers, and work extended in its hours to cover many of the hours that people at other companies would have considered social time. One of the things I liked was that the company was full of incredibly bright, interesting people who were fascinated by the same subjects I was fascinated with, which were computers and operating systems.

After I'd been at Microsoft a few months, I missed something. At college, which was full of equally bright people, there was a diversity of interests. I had friends who were musicians and scholars of literature and actors and chemists and mathematicians. At Microsoft, while there were a number of people who were interested in those disciplines on an amateur level, everybody was primarily focused on computers and computation. While those are and were fascinating to me, they weren't the whole of my interests. I spent a long time at Microsoft missing the broader community of scholars in a variety of disciplines. Since leaving Microsoft and going back to the university, of course I miss the incredibly focused group of very bright people who are interested in computers.

I have never encountered a brighter group of people than at Microsoft. If you're an intellectual and your brain is your primary play toy, you like to masturbate with your head instead of your hands. There's nothing more fun than being surrounded by bright people whom you can jive off of and play and explore bizarre ideas. What would it take to commercialize cat milk? How long would it take, what would you need? Could you use genetic engineering? What about mechanical aids? That's a typical Microsoft conversation. At least for me. Some people probably discuss professional sports.

After a few years, I made friends outside the company, many at the University of Washington as I began to date a student there, which enormously expanded my social circle. I met people who weren't programming computers 60 to 80 hours a week, and maybe didn't even deal with computers professionally. There was often difficulty integrating non-Microsoft people into my social life, partly because of the incredible lack of social skills that many developers had. For example, many people might need *context* to understand a discussion of the relative merits of the DEC VAX 780 versus the Altair (the VAX ruled).

✦

As I understand the law, lots of things that are legal for a company when they are not a monopoly become illegal when they are a monopoly. The difficulty with this, of course, is determining when your company is a monopoly. I'm not a lawyer.

If you're the CEO of a major company and you suspect you may be running a monopoly, you should talk to your corporate counsel, but here are some of the things you should watch out for:

1. Do you have any competitors, that is, does anyone sell a product or service which could replace yours? For example, if you sell a Web browser, does anyone else sell one? Of course, you might be giving away your product, and then you'd have to ask if anyone else was giving away a similar product, though the whole notion of illegal gift monopolies seems odd to me. "Let's prosecute these people for giving away something better than what these other people are giving away. The consumer is being hurt by all this free software! Make them pay!"

2. Are there huge barriers to entry in your marketplace, like stringing wires through a city or obtaining rights of way for your railroad tracks, or could a bunch of graduate students produce a serious competitor to your products, like an operating system or a Web browser?

3. Does your product have a geologic source such that ownership of those lands would allow you to control the world's supply of your product, like oil or diamonds? Redmond is a nice town, but a lot of software gets written in other places like Silicon Valley.

Now, if any of the above three points are true, you might have a monopoly. If you do, then lots of what you used to do in competition with other companies just became illegal. If Microsoft is a monopoly, then it is probable that some of its hardball tactics are illegal because of that fact. But I have a hard time seeing how it is a monopoly when the barriers to entry in the software business are such that unorganized volunteers can write products that threaten Microsoft's market share.

Microsoft has always been a very tough competitor. The sales and marketing people I knew were just as driven as the developers. I never saw anything that would be illegal in a non-monopolistic situation, just fierce determination to win market share.

The antitrust lawsuit has had two effects on me: it precipitated a decline in the stock price that fed into the bursting of the Internet bubble, so I lost some money, and it caused people who know I worked for Microsoft to ask me detailed legal questions about the Sherman Antitrust Act of 1890.

Luckily, my education has rendered me unable to answer these questions sensibly, so I am free to make up long metaphoric answers relating antitrust law to Peruvian cooking. "Picture, if you will, a company as a stuffed guinea pig, roasting in the oven. If there is only one guinea pig in the oven, will everyone get enough meat at the meal?" One or two of these explanations and word gets around at the party to steer clear of the topic with me.

As for Microsoft's reputation changing from The Little Company That Took On IBM to Satan's Tool Of World Domination, a few people seemed to feel that I was personally responsible. Unfortunately, none of them were in management positions at Microsoft granting me more stock options.

The husband of one college friend wrote me a letter in broken English claiming that the French Macintosh version of Microsoft Word was an attempt to destroy French sovereignty. I never quite made out his reasoning, but I assured him that I, personally, had no interest in destroying French sovereignty, as I was neither German nor a

McDonald's stockholder.

Occasionally, at parties, drunks berate me for killing WordStar or Lotus 1-2-3, but I always tell them I'm retired now and working for my favorite charity, Handguns for the Homeless. ("The less you own, the more important it is to protect it.") That's usually inflammatory enough that they change the subject.

✦

Losing my identity as a Microsoft programmer was very hard, more difficult than I expected. When I left Microsoft at the age of 37, I went off to school and was surrounded by people twenty years younger.

I was suddenly a novice again. These people are half my age, they think faster than I do, and they're extraordinarily photogenic and witty and full of improvisational comedy. I feel really old, stupid, and slow.

I am pursuing a degree in Drama, a subject utterly removed from my degree in Computer Science. I was pig-ignorant of the ways of the theater, and a freshman. I've been studying drama in order to write screenplays and plays. They're better to write than novels because they have very wide margins, lots of white space, and no descriptions of furniture.

People ask me why I'm attending the University of Washington. It's simple: the UW was the only major university within walking distance of my house and I had just bought a new dishwasher. I know it's embarrassing to make major life decisions based on appliances, but this wasn't like a toaster oven, or some other little appliance, this was a big built-in. For my first eight years at Microsoft, I didn't own a car and I rode the bus everywhere. I chose my house to be very close to the direct bus line to Microsoft, which turned out to be a fairly nice neighborhood close to the university.

Travel is the other thing I've done since leaving the company. I've taken a few quarters off from the university and traveled with my wife. In the last two years, we've gone to Canada, England, and we'll say Scotland, because it might be a separate country, and Ireland, and

France, Italy, Peru, Ecuador, China, Japan, New Zealand, and Australia. We've traveled in a comfortable but not extravagant style in accordance with our wealth—typically no more than 30 or 40 porters. We rarely take the grand, usually just the upright piano, although it was *incredibly* difficult getting it on the Chunnel train.

✦

The money has permitted me to travel and to work by choice, which are the two greatest freedoms I can imagine. We only get one life and it's not a hypothetical exercise.

I don't have to work, which is extraordinary enough, and if I'm prudent, my children won't either. (Although I'll require them to work for the food we serve them. At very low cost; not much profit built in.)

Not so strangely, I find that my tastes and psychology of spending are still close to my upbringing. I worry about how much money I spend, I haunt used bookstores instead of new bookstores, I think about saving electricity and not using much gas. $10 here and $10 there seem to add up to me. I believe this is called neurosis in mental health circles.

My most recent housemate was a third-grade teacher. I liked living with him; he was a great guy and a lot of fun. He recently married and moved out, but one of the things he said was that he liked me because I wasn't one of those evil Microsoft millionaires driving up the housing market. I live in the same shabby dwelling I had purchased when I was a young engineer, I drive an old Honda Civic, and I live approximately as simply as I always had, although I think my roommate overlooked the extraordinary luxury of my not working.

The self-pity of the rich is a fairly disgusting idea, but one of the difficulties that I and many of my friends have is deciding how to give our lives significance. Most people work to feed, clothe, and house themselves. If you're free from that, you're left with a large part of your waking hours to be filled. It took a certain amount of ambition, or at least diligence, to succeed at Microsoft, to remain there long enough to receive enough money that you would no longer have to work. So the people who've left Microsoft generally want to achieve something.

Most of the people I know create artificial structures to fill their time, artificial in the sense that they aren't needed for survival. They center their lives around their children's lives, which can be scary. They center their lives around community service, they center their lives around jobs they don't need. They start companies, they join companies. One friend set out to become a concert clarinetist. I have a friend who wants a museum. She's working very hard to build it. I want one too, but not enough to work full-time for it.

Some, like me, go back to school. But you have to decide: what am I going to do and why am I going to do it? Why aren't I living purely for pleasure? Why don't I sit on the porch, drink gin, and shoot squirrels? There's no reason in the world, except my own psychology, which prevents me from doing that.

It's a harder problem than it seems. But it's a problem I wish everyone could have. It haunts one. It's a deep one: if I could do anything in the world, what would I do? There are those who set out on hopeless, quixotic tasks. Do we feel guilt at our wealth that we wish to expiate by serving others? Or are we just bored?

David Hare said that the rich suffer from the illusion that they must have once done something right. Some Microsoft employees believe that they are deserving of their wealth. The wealth was correlated—but not proportionally correlated—with the effort they expended.

Anyone who feels a moral righteousness because of the long hours isn't in touch with how the rest of the world works. I worked hard, but no harder than my friends at Digital Equipment Corporation, or IBM, or medieval history graduate school, or comparative literature graduate school, or for that matter, farming or mining in Zambia, or any of a thousand ways of earning a living.

I had a discussion with an older friend of mine, a very conservative man who'd never given to charity in his life. He asked me why I gave to charity. I said I had a vision of the world that I wanted to live in, and I was willing to pay for it. The way to pay for it was not to buy a bigger car or a house in a gated community, but to support causes that try to change the world.

I'm struck by people who vote against increases in property taxes because they have no school-age children. I wonder whether they realize that if they don't educate the children of their neighbors, the world they live in as they age will be far less pleasant, not only for those children, but for them?

Technology has improved the lives of the vast majority of people in the first world. Sanitation and vaccination have increased our life span, as have, to a lesser extent, antibiotics. Central heating, hot running water, electric light, these things all make life more comfortable.

The way you get technology is to educate people so they grow up to produce technology, which leads me to believe that if I want advances in technology that will make my life more pleasant, I should support the education of the people who will produce the technology of the future. The same is true for the arts. If I want to turn on the radio in thirty years and hear Bach, I should support the education of people who will perform Bach, and the education of people who create a demand for performances of Bach.

We as a society have a duty to distribute the excess wealth we generate, whether it be in the enormous magnitude of Microsoft wealth or ordinary middle-class income. Even if you operate purely from self-interest, an educated, vaccinated civil society is far better to live in than a gated community where you exclude those people you deem undesirable. I would argue that we are better off making our neighbors desirable instead of excluding the undesirable among them.

But the best part about having worked for Microsoft—better than the money, better than the intellectual challenge, better even than playing a small part in the computer revolution—is providing computer support for all one's aged relatives.

There's nothing as heartwarming as an early Sunday morning phone call from Aunt Mildred:

"Why has that little thing gone to the side and won't move, even when I press the key? The key the man on the phone told me to press last time I called about that other problem. Could this be a virus? I was using my files. The one with the little boxes along the top that change things. Maybe that email from Ted about Doris's surgery had a virus. Did you get that? I took out the disk, but now nothing shows up, but I have to print a letter to Joan Widdleson. She moved to Des Moines because Cindy was in medical school near there and had a baby, but her husband, Cindy's husband, has a job, maybe in a law firm or accounting or something like that where they dress nicer, and they didn't want daycare, but now the pumpkin bread recipe is stuck inside the Internet. Anyway, every time I press the key, the computer gives me this message about the open thing, but the printer only does the first page of the other disk with the pictures of Sue, but the colors are wrong.

"Can you help me?"

Reanne

Always warm, chatty, and interested in other people, Ava Reanne had a unique overview of the company's administrative side; in fact, she started many of the processes and groups that exist today. A little older than the average employee, blue-eyed and auburn haired, she was a buddy to many and a motherly figure to some. She comments on Microsoft's growing pains and its evolution as she worked alongside the top executives in the company. Those of you with packed schedules will laugh when you see what Steve Ballmer does when he's late for a plane.

In 1981 I was a 39-year-old mother of three in desperate need of a job. My family had moved to Seattle the year before from California for my husband's job, which now no longer existed. I had experience as an Activities Director for a nursing home, a substitute teacher, a teacher's aide, an Activities Coordinator at the Cleveland Society for the Blind, in activities at a state mental hospital, and lastly as an office worker for a wholesale plant distributor. My sole exposure to computers was in the last position, where we could see a computer through a glass office partition.

In Seattle I applied to a placement agency, took their tests, and interviewed for a couple of jobs. I was told by the agency that one of the companies I interviewed for was moving very fast, had very smart people, and didn't want to take much time with the interviews. Essentially, they were looking for a general office person who was smart and could work without much direction. The position involved answering the main switchboard, reception, and providing general support for various work groups. There were about 90 people in the company, mostly under 30 years of age, and they were located in two buildings in downtown Bellevue. [If you thought Microsoft was in Seattle, you're not alone. The main campus is east of Seattle, separated by a long bridge across Lake Washington.]

I prepared for the interview by developing a two-paragraph résumé. I figured nothing I could put on it about my other jobs was relevant; I just needed to convince them that I could do the job. At the interview, I talked with about seven people in 45 minutes.

When the agency got back to me, they said that I would need to talk with Bill Gates before I could be hired and that I was the only one they were considering at this point. I waited three weeks. The agency had to keep convincing me that this was the place I should work. Waiting was hard for a family with no income!

I later found out that Microsoft's expectations were fairly low, as I was replacing a gal who was let go because she wouldn't put her shoes on to greet guests. Finally, I received the call to come in to talk with Bill. I was hired and started the following week.

Steve and Bill were hiring software engineers from various college campuses. Since I supported them in this, I was tasked with getting the students in for interviews, making hotel reservations, scheduling hosts for lunch and dinner, and following the results of the day of interviews. If the person was hired, I assisted with the move and found temporary housing once they arrived.

I was not always sure that everyone would remember to be there for early morning interviews. If an interviewer didn't show up, I had to quickly find another person to talk with our candidate. Once someone forgot he was to take a candidate for lunch. He called me and said he could do it, but did I think the candidate would mind if he stopped by his home to pick up some shoes? Well, I did manage to keep my shoes on, but not everyone at Microsoft was required to do so!

Another time, Mark, a software engineer, dressed up in a gorilla suit to tease Steve. Steve greatly disappointed him when the gorilla approached him in the hall and Steve kept a straight face while walking by him saying, "Hi, Mark!" This was also an interview day for the developer. He had forgotten, but he decided to have some fun with the candidate. When the candidate was escorted to the office, Mark was sitting there in the gorilla suit working on his computer. I'm sure that was one memorable interview.

✦

Organization was my greatest skill and I found my job challenging and fun. I met all the people hired for technical jobs during the early years and got to know the managers who did the interviewing. In the next few years, the company grew from 90 to over 500 employees. The Campus Recruiting program grew and each year we sent more and more technical people to the campuses to interview. Being busy and focused caused some unique situations with the travel to college campuses.

I remember one time that Steve Ballmer and Charles Simonyi were in Boston interviewing at MIT and Harvard. We had just moved into a new building and were working with new phones, our first mail stops, new support staff in reception, and so forth.

I was following up on a technical interview when Bill's secretary handed me a frantic call from Steve. He was at the Boston airport and couldn't find Charles and the plane was about to leave. At the same time, a call came in from Charles. I took his call and found that he was also in the airport looking for Steve. I now had them both on the phone and had to decide whether to interpret directions for each of them, or to try to use the conference feature on the phone for the first time and risk losing them both! Whew, the conference call worked, and they got home on time.

Steve and Bill traveled the red-eye in coach, changing into business attire in the airport and arriving just in time for early morning meetings on the east coast. They often found themselves arriving at planes just before the doors closed. Twice Steve cut his time so short that he left the rental car in the airport departure lanes. When he got back from those trips, he told me, "Oh, yeah. Call the rental car place and tell them where the car is." Making their travel arrangements was often a full-time job.

✦

Microsoft moved from one office building to another very fast in those early years. We moved into the Northup Building from the two downtown office buildings as our first of many, many office moves. Steve arranged all the details with the moving company and the technical staff so that the move could be made over the weekend and people could set up their offices and get back to work on Monday. Only weekend work time would be lost! This first move was very disruptive, but over the years subsequent office moves became more routine.

Steve, Bill, Paul Allen, and the other managers set up the office so that most everyone had equal status—no fancy offices, everyone did their own copy work, answered their phones, traveled coach, etc. In the Northup Building, most every employee now had his/her own office, but not everyone had a window office. It was decided that those with seniority got the window offices, and this was not necessarily the managers. That changed over the years, and managers eventually got the windows even if they didn't have seniority.

Each week the company changed in some respect. There were new phones, but no one had thought about how the phone numbers were to be assigned and the system was set up so that each phone number corresponded to the person's office number. Right away that caused problems, as within two weeks groups of people were moving offices as new hires came in. The phone system was changed so that the phone number was linked to the person. Sure made it easier on the switchboard operator and receptionist.

The third day after the move to Northup, I noticed five or six mail bags tossed in a corner of the warehouse. I asked someone what was happening with the mail. No one had told the warehouse people what to do with it, and since they were so busy, it was being stored there. You can imagine what Steve's reaction was to this, and I quickly organized the first mail stops at Microsoft.

I once commented, jokingly, that I had experience in working with the mentally ill and the blind, which eminently qualified me for understanding how to work with people at Microsoft. I was specifically referring to the fact that I found many of managers and technical people to be socially inept—you know, the usual thing of looking people in the eye, and saying "Hi!" when you passed in the hall was missing. They had gotten into the business of Microsoft so deeply that they barely acknowledged that other people existed.

Communication was beginning to be difficult as the hiring increased. Early on, we used two separate email systems and you had to know which system a person was on to send email.

I suggested a company newsletter. Steve said, "Sure, why don't you go ahead and start it and see how everyone responds?" I said, "Okay, maybe I'll have time for that every other week or so." I got it started and soon Steve was saying that I *had* to get the MicroNews out *every* Monday, as everyone expected it. We asked people what they would like to see in the newsletter and eventually included company news, stories about what people were doing as volunteers, new hire announcements, group changes, and even a classified section. My job changed almost weekly, but I continued with the newsletter for almost a year before someone else took over.

In order to keep everyone updated with Microsoft's role in what was happening in the computer industry, Steve and Bill decided to hold company meetings every six months. And you guessed it, I was to find a place that would hold everyone, set up a date and time, set up the room, and see that everyone had a copy of the agenda for the meeting. And oh, yes, contact the speakers and make sure they were fully prepared for their presentations.

As the company grew, Microsoft switched to annual company meetings, the meetings got bigger and more complicated, and finally an agency was hired to coordinate the event. Finding locations also became difficult and the Seattle Convention Center and the Arena at Seattle Center have been used. What's next? Maybe the football stadium?

Other events were always happening. Birthdays were often celebrated in the work groups, but some were company events; Steve was presented with a big cake and a special singing telegram one year. When the first version of Excel shipped, there was a big party to celebrate. The cake was supposed to look like an Excel product box. In order to get that particular shade of green, an awful lot of green dye was used in the frosting. It was a great cake, but soon people noticed others' green tongues and mouths. We all had the mark of Excel by the time we realized what was happening. The ones in special trouble were those who were going on dates that Friday night. I think they had some " 'splaining" to do!

December Holiday Parties were always very special, with lots of food and great entertainment. That first one in the Northup Building was one that I will never forget. There were about 150 people on board that December and this party was just a casual get-together prior to the 24th.

We set up in the lobby with the food tables about six feet in front of the elevators. Tables and chairs and the kegs were set up in the big unfinished area just off the lobby. We decorated the tables and everything looked festive. Pizza arrived and people began to wander down to see what was happening.

It was a good time: beer flowed, people chatted, and Bill started jumping. He was talking with a group of people when he said he could jump over the table. Of course he was challenged, and he jumped. And made it from where he was standing.

A little later, Bill came out near the tables to get more pizza. No one was paying much attention to him until he backed up a little getting ready to jump the food table. Everyone was paying attention by then and was telling him, "No!" and "Yes! Go for it!" and "Not the pizza!" Bill jumped, turned to grin, and backed into the opening elevator doors. As he fell into the elevator, the doors closed and took him to the second floor. When he came out, everyone cheered and he gave a rather shy bow!

✦

The one thing we could always count on was that nothing would stay the same—each day, week, month, and year brought more changes than we could count. I found myself confronting new situations and people continually. It made me really look at myself and discover new internal resources as well as areas that I seriously needed to work on.

One big lesson I learned at Microsoft was how to let go of things, people, and jobs. If you do a job long enough, that job can become who you are. We all know there is more to us than our job identity, but we don't truly learn that lesson until we have to give up parts of the job. The day someone took over the company newsletter, the day someone took over the personnel records, the day someone became Steve's personal assistant, the day someone was hired for campus recruiting—all these were necessary for the growth of the company.

I didn't always see these changes as contributing to my growth, but they did. I always had a challenging job with smart people. I had lost sight of how challenging the job was and how smart the people were until I left and had to work with people in the real world!

I probably wouldn't be hired at Microsoft today, an irony I can enjoy now. However, I do really appreciate the lessons presented by eleven years of working there. In January '93, I ended my 30-year marriage, left Microsoft, and moved to Minneapolis, Minnesota.

I spent the next five years learning more about myself and about relationships. I remarried and started a Shiatsu massage business as well as teaching Namakoshi Shiatsu. When my husband and I retired in the summer of '97, we relocated to Reno, Nevada to be nearer family. We are comfortably enjoying life, our families, and traveling; all things I didn't take the time to do when working at Microsoft.

Of all the time I value at Microsoft, I especially value that one performance review when Steve had to talk me into taking some stock rather than an increase in my hourly rate!

Jack

Jack is friendly, talkative, strong-willed, and assertive. Unruly brown hair can't hide his deep blue eyes and it's hard to catch him with his shirt tucked in. Unless you're already an industry expert, his many years of watching the rise and fall of various tech players will give you insight into the roots of power struggles that are continuing to play out now. If Jack had his way, this chapter would be numerically oriented and techie to the point of unreadability by the rest of us. He was one of the in crowd, always nearby when there was unicycle jousting to be done or pranks to be pulled.

My connection to Microsoft came through a friend, John, from a previous job in Massachusetts. Steve Ballmer told John that they were looking for a compiler person who knew UNIX, and John immediately thought of me.

I knew about Microsoft and its 8080 Basic software. I was a compiler guy, and like most "real" computer science people I didn't have much respect for Basic. I also was in the middle of a big project at work and wasn't really thinking about changing jobs at the time. But I'd always liked the Seattle area and it was a chance to travel and to visit a friend, so I took the opportunity.

Since I didn't need the job, I was relaxed and did well in the interviews. Bill Gates made me an offer on the spot. I told Steve and Bill that I was in the middle of a project and wouldn't leave it until it was ready to be turned over to someone else, and they approved of that loyalty. My friend John was also offered a job, but didn't take it. About a year later, he wound up going to a little startup in Silicon Valley: Sun Microsystems.

Within a few months of the job offer, some big changes happened at my old company that left me less happy, and I decided to join Microsoft. I spent the month of July 1981 driving across the country, camping and hiking along the way.

I'd spent the night before showing up for my new job in a rest stop, and hadn't had a shower for about a week because I'd been backpacking in Glacier Park in Montana. I didn't remember exactly where Microsoft was (confused by the fact that there are two streets named 8th in Bellevue), but I finally found the building and went up to the 8th floor.

I walked past the receptionist like I knew what I was doing and wandered around until I found someone I knew, which was Bill Gates. He called Ballmer and while we waited for Steve to arrive, Bill explained that they'd been a little worried. I'd been completely out of contact while I was driving across the country, and had turned off the telephone and moved out of my apartment. Apparently my itinerary had gotten garbled and all they knew was that my stuff had arrived but that there was no sign of me.

Steve took me to his office right away and had me sign contracts and non-disclosures and such. He was really excited about something and wanted me to see. He took me into a tiny closet that had a small table, a chair, many boxes, and the card cage of a machine.

It was the regular rectangular shape of most of the 8080 desktop machines of the day, and had a couple of 5-inch floppy drives on the front. But instead of the usual S100 bus, the processor was on the motherboard, which also had expansion slots for what looked like oversized Apple II cards. It used the 8086/88 chip, which was the worst of the new 16-bit processors, but I recognized they'd copied the best of

Apple's ideas and added a few of their own. There was no sign of a manufacturer's logo anywhere on the machine, but Steve told me who it was: IBM. About a month later an actor playing Charlie Chaplin's Little Tramp character presented the new computer to the world.

This machine defined the personal computer standard. Only IBM could have forced this new standard on the world, and only IBM would have been as widely accepted by non-computer people. 90% of the personal computers built to this day remain compatible with it.

✦

The IBM PC's popularity also strengthened the feud between Microsoft and the homebrewers.

Back in the mid '70s, the company that evolved into Microsoft had written most of the systems software for the first real personal computer, the MITS Altair. Because it was possible, many of the customers of the Altair and its successors did not pay Microsoft (or anyone else) for their software, but copied it. They took it as a mark of pride and a sign of the superiority of the technology that they could do this. But it meant that software developers weren't getting paid for their work.

Bill Gates wrote an open letter to the Homebrew Computer Club, which complained about this fact. The homebrewers never forgave him.

It's important to understand this in the context of the times. All of the homebrewers, including Bill and Paul (and me) were hippies at some level. A big part of the hippie movement was the principal of sharing—that everything should be available to everyone for free.

To the homebrewers, the computer could be a positive contribution to this vision: it was easy to share software, data, printers, everything. You still had to buy hardware, which the new microcomputer technologies were making cheaper every day, but the rest, the important parts, the software, could be free as the air.

At the time, most computers were owned by big, faceless corporations and were used to do big, faceless things. But the homebrewers knew that it didn't need to be that way, and they were doing their part by brewing up their own computers at home.

Ted Nelson came along with his hypertext idea at about the same time, and showed how with fairly simple network hardware and a simple protocol you could not only share all data, but do it in a smart way that expanded its power enormously. All the homebrewers got his point immediately and it added to their vision of the wonderful future. Today we know Ted Nelson's idea as the World Wide Web.

We all knew that the personal computer would be a wonderful, revolutionary thing and would change the world in ways that would be good for almost everyone. Besides, they were fun to play with. For more on this story, check out Ted Nelson's *Computer Lib/Dream Machines*, and Steven Levy's *Hackers*. Both are excellent books.

Very few of the homebrewers cared about money, and very few of them had any. A few were trying to run businesses, nearly all of them selling hardware, and most were losing money. So the idea that software could be free was very attractive to them. But with his open letter, Bill threw cold water on the fire. The homebrewers resented him all the more because he had a point. They called him names, the worst of which associated him with IBM.

In the 50s through 70s, IBM was the most dominant monopoly in the history of the computer industry. They sold something like 90% of all computers, 98% of all corporate computers, and something like 70% of all software used in the free world. They had their own way of doing things, and they defended their monopoly aggressively, ruthlessly, and with dirty tricks. "No one ever got fired for choosing IBM" was not just an advertising slogan; until about 1980, it was a fact. People often did get in trouble, including sometimes being fired, for choosing a competitor.

The most interesting competition IBM had was Digital Equipment Corporation, which made a big point of making friends with academic computer scientists. DEC carved a niche for itself making small computers, making a point of not trying to compete with IBM head on.

The homebrew people nearly all came from the DEC side of the computer world, and they hated IBM. IBM stood for everything they were against: big, corporate, faceless, mean, expensive, inflexible, etc. In short, the Evil Empire. DEC, with its academic bent, encouraged outsiders, especially universities, to write software for their machines and much of it was distributed freely, particularly within the academic community. DEC fit in perfectly with the hippie sensibilities of the homebrewers.

In 1980, some guys in the unmistakable dark blue suits of IBM turned up at Microsoft. Since the fewer than 30 Microsoft employees at the time already had more work than they could handle, Bill thought he'd spread the wealth around a little by sending IBM to his friend Gary Kildall, who had written CP/M, the leading operating system for the 8080 processor. Gary ran a company called Intergalactic Digital Research, Inc. (Later they dropped the "Intergalactic" part.)

When the suits arrived at Digital Research, Kildall happened to be out of the office and the receptionist had them wait in the lobby. Apparently she'd been listening when the programmers said nasty things about IBM, and rather than telling the IBMers the truth, she played along with the culture and was rude to them and didn't tell them that the boss was out of the office and couldn't be reached. After several hours of this abuse they left, refusing to go back, and they wound up buying an operating system from Microsoft.

When the IBM PC came out in the summer of 1981, the homebrew side of the world saw Microsoft's affiliation with them as traitorous and proof that Bill Gates was evil, just as they'd suspected after the open letter. In fact, Microsoft continued to do things homebrew style, mostly using DEC development hosts and DEC-style standards, flying in the face of everything IBM stood for. Mainstream IBM hated it, couldn't understand it, and couldn't adapt to it.

Nevertheless, the IBM PC very quickly became completely dominant in the microcomputer market, and in fact, created markets that had never existed before, just as Bill and its backers at IBM knew it would. While the mainstream IBMers couldn't argue with success, they were careful to keep the new system and its people isolated lest they contaminate the rest of IBM.

Then a tragedy happened. Don Estridge, the IBM "radical" who had understood how important personal computers would be and had forced the thing through IBM management despite incredible resistance, was killed in an airplane crash. Estridge's replacement proved to be spectacularly shortsighted. He tried to force the PC world to go back to the IBM way of doing things, and in his disastrous failure to do so, opened the door for Microsoft.

The divorce that occurred between Microsoft and IBM in 1990 was a gamble for Microsoft, but Microsoft won, and the image of Microsoft as the Giant Killer was impossible to avoid. Until that time, Microsoft had always been one of the bigger microcomputer software companies, but companies like VisiCorp, Lotus, Digital Research, and a few others had been bigger. (Compared to the mainframe software companies, all were tiny. In fact, until 1997, IBM's revenue from software *alone* was larger than Microsoft's entire gross.) But in the mid 80s through early 90s, each of the competitors made some enormous stumble or other, and all fell by the wayside. Microsoft, with superior diversification, was better able to recover from its many stumbles.

The homebrewers and their kindred ended up starting and working for companies like Apple, Digital Research, Sun Microsystems, and Lotus, and quite a few even came to Microsoft. You don't hear Steve Wozniak [founder and principal techie at Apple] or Andy Bechtolshein [developer of the original SUN computer and founder of Sun Microsystems] railing against Microsoft.

Most of the homebrewers understood what was really happening, but the people who joined their companies later were like the receptionist at Digital Research. They were steeped in the culture of hating IBM and its supposed minion, and of course they resented losing the battle when their companies stumbled. But rather than trying to figure out why they'd lost, and competing harder and better in the next battle, they turned their resentment into hatred and began lobbying for a legal remedy. Sadly, some of the latecomers at Microsoft gave them ammunition.

When the Republicans started screaming about dubious political contributions to the Democratic party and accusing the Justice Department of not doing enough to investigate, the administration copied the Republican strategy of distractions, and came up with a distraction of their own: they would go after Microsoft. It worked.

I'm very irritated at the salesmen who provoked the suit, who, having had their hands slapped once, came back and did it again. The technical merits of the suit are complex: the browser *is* an integral part of the rest of the system, and for good reasons, and there's no way to actually remove it without emasculating the system (although it's easy to take the icon off the desktop). For example, the Help system and the browser or viewer features of a number of applications use Internet Explorer internals. These things wouldn't work if Explorer were removed.

On the other hand, there were members of the sales force that were needlessly cutthroat. Microsoft would have done just fine without the unfair bundling that was the main element of the first suit and the only element of merit in the second. The salespeople wouldn't have gotten as big a commission, that's all.

The salesmen went up against Netscape and exploited its vulnerabilities ruthlessly until it fell. It was not necessary. Netscape would have either gone away or diversified or merged with somebody. The browser/http server business was never lucrative enough to support a big company on its own. Netscape benefitted from being near the front of an important innovation and the related stock market boom. They were lucky AOL bought them before the boom ended or they'd probably have folded in a pretty dramatic way.

Microsoft made Netscape's business more difficult, but it certainly didn't kill them. I'll stop short of saying that competition from Microsoft was a blessing in disguise, but without that competition, their stock price would have remained at absurd levels until the collapse came and it would have been tough for another company to absorb them. They might have been able to diversify into enough other businesses to survive, but they've showed no particular talent for it.

One of my biggest irritations is that the priority at Microsoft has shifted over the years away from technical merit toward shallow salesmaking. The "Mac-ification" of Windows is a perfect example. The supposedly soft and friendly Windows interface actually makes it more difficult to get inside the machine and do sophisticated computer-nerd tasks. The interface, which looks like an inferior clone of the Macintosh, is easier for non-computer people at the expense of the techies who want to go deeper. So Windows opens MS to criticism from both extremes.

Compared to what IBM did in the old days, or what the Baby Bells are doing now, Microsoft's monopolistic behavior, while real, is minor and a red herring. The IBM of the old days would, for example, market products that were only a gleam in some salesman's eye and they wouldn't begin development until they had enough interest that they thought it would pay. Since there's no development overhead with this approach, they could move very fast when a competitor seemed to be encroaching somewhere. Eventually this practice was made illegal, but not before they did a lot of damage. There were lots of other abuses, and nothing Microsoft has done comes close.

The good news is that Enron and their ilk have raised public awareness of the seriousness of real corporate abuses. Microsoft's abuses are obviously minor by comparison.

✦

When I started in the summer of '81, there were about 80 employees, including about 50 developers. The rest were tech writers, salespeople, receptionists, and one accountant. A lawyer was hired the next year. Steve Ballmer did all recruiting, although that fall he hired someone to help him.

In those days a peon developer reported to a nominal manager (who was also a full-time techie), who reported to Bill—a pretty flat structure. In fact, a tremendous amount of intergroup communication came about because Paul Allen would wander around in the middle of the night and talk to people. It was typical for quite a few people to be there at 4 a.m. and sometimes we'd go to a nearby Denny's for ice cream. We didn't have schedules. What we did have looked more like a list of priorities (which would change very often) and a deadline. We'd do whatever we could in the time available, and most of us were highly motivated to do the job right. We all knew what that meant and nobody needed to manage us or our time.

All the developers worked on a mainframe computer, either a PDP-11/70 or a DEC 20/60 (these are both what were called "superminis"). The targets we were developing for were all "little" computers, so we had to download our software each time we wanted to run it on the target. We spent as much time using the big machine as we could, since the tools on the target were always minimal or nonexistent. We were generally writing them ourselves as we went along.

My group, which was developing the Xenix operating system, had mandatory team lunches once a week. We always went to a restaurant, most often Chinese. We'd all bundle into the largest car. We all had small foreign cars and most were quite beat up, including mine, the Entropymobile. When we couldn't fit into two cars, the lunches stopped entirely and we started having our meetings in conference rooms like normal people. Start of a long downhill slide.

By 1986 the company had over 1,000 employees and there was real bureaucracy. Of those 1,000 employees, probably fewer than 300 were developers. There was another big change afoot: for the first time, it was becoming reasonable to put a machine running DOS, or the new system, OS/2, on every desk, and expect that to be the employee's primary computer, be they developers or paper-pushers.

This idea, which eventually became known as "eating your own dog food," took a long time to catch on. Having to use the operating system you were developing *as you were creating it* can be a difficult thing to do. The Xenix group did it very early, but of course we had a pretty reasonable platform, with networking, compilers, mailers, and so on, right from the start. In '84 the Windows group had begun using a variety of networks, including Novell's twisted pair system, and deserve credit as the number two group to eat their own dog food, developing under DOS.

But they still had to keep their connections to one of the big machines to run email and do backups, just like the other people doing development for DOS and other small systems, as well as the non-programmers. When Microsoft's third operating system, OS/2, came out in '87, these things became viable on the local machine, and the end of Xenix was in sight. Management decided to get out of the Xenix business, even though it was quite profitable for very little effort. They felt it was too confusing for customers to have to choose from three different systems.

By the way, Windows for Xenix was started, headway made, and then killed, three separate times. A lot of us mourned the loss of Xenix, as it was a significantly better system than anything else the company has ever done—more efficient (by a lot!), more stable, more internally consistent, and for a very long time, more advanced—but politics won the day.

A couple of years later, we held a wake, and nearly everyone who had ever worked on Xenix showed up, including quite a few who had gone to competitors or development partners. For those of us that saw the point, it was a frustrating experience to see such a good product choked off in its prime, but that's life, I guess. It's not the only time it happened at Microsoft.

By that point, there were very few one-person projects anymore, but most of them still had only about three to eight developers, including a lead. Development projects tended to take a year to 18 months from inception to shipping, where five years earlier, six months would have been considered a long-term project.

By the mid 80s, a lot of us had families, where in the early 80s, almost no one did. Very few people worked more than a 60-hour week, except when the crunch came. We socialized with other Microsoft people still, but we were all getting involved in other activities besides work. We had mortgages, dependents, and retirement plans. A new experience.

Nowadays, there are very few projects that involve fewer than 500 people, with fewer than 20% of those being developers. To be sure, each little component has its own small team and some of them have only one developer, but it's very rare for a single developer to create a whole product that's marketed on its own, where that had been the norm in the early 80s. Development cycles are generally about three years. For example, Windows 98 was started fairly early in '95 and shipped in late '98, and it was an update, not even a new product.

The development systems today are far more sophisticated than the separate editors, compilers, linkers, and assembly debuggers we used before, but this comes at a price. Today most products are built using large libraries; some general purpose, some special purpose for the product.

The overhead of these libraries is enormous, using up 70–95% of the disk image and execution time of the product. This and other factors tend to make fatter, less efficient code. Very, very few of the developers hired by Microsoft in the '90s have written a single line of assembly language, where a decade earlier, everyone was fluent in it and a lot of people used it exclusively.

As a result of this change in perspective, most developers today are unaware of the loss in efficiency they're causing. It's a truism of engineering that the organization of a project tends to resemble the team that put it together. Because there are many levels of management now, there is a tremendous overhead in interfaces and redundancy that wouldn't exist in a smaller project.

In my last job at Microsoft, there were eight levels between the CEO and me (non-inclusive); most of them were relatively non-technical and tended to run things by checking off milestones on a schedule rather than actually understanding the significance of what was being accomplished. We'd become a typical big company.

At every level, the underlings are motivated to satisfy the schedule rather than to do the job right, often by inflating their accomplishments. The overlings then require them to move on to the next thing on the schedule, irrespective of the actual status or quality of the component or the wisdom of a schedule written years earlier. The underlings always hope to get a moment in edgewise to clean things up, but they never do.

✦

There are a lot of nice things about having been a part of the company when it was small. For example, one time I came back to the office just in time to be in the elevator when they shut the power off. While I was stuck in there in the dark, halfway between floors, I overheard the guys in the lobby talking about why they'd shut the power off: there was a fire in the building's power transformer.

Naturally, I tried to climb out through the hatch, but they'd locked it (state law, it turns out). Being stuck in an elevator when there's a fire opens your eyes to some things. I haven't completely stopped using elevators, but never for trips of less than about five floors.

Many modern building designs focus on using the elevator, and the stairs are put into out-of-the-way corners. When my office was moved to a building in which the stairs were quite effectively hidden, it took me more than a week to track down the optimal route from underground parking to my office using the stairs, and the route was pretty long. Using the elevator, it would be easy. But I wasn't interested in using the elevator for such a short trip.

So I had a long discussion with one of my old friends in facilities. He agreed with my points, and since he happened to be involved with the design of what was to become the standard Microsoft building, this became an important design element. All the new buildings have a stairway at each end of each main corridor with big windows all around. They're impossible to miss. It also turns out that the landings are pretty big, so people go to the stairway to have hallway meetings and look at the view. By the way, *far* more is accomplished in hallway meetings than in meeting-room meetings.

✦

Random programming story: one time, I was trying to get a compiler to self-compile. There was a particular bug that involved several very large trees in memory simultaneously, and a pointer was getting trashed mysteriously. The minimum case was very big and complex and I just couldn't figure it out. I'd spent all day, something like 15 hours, staring at this thing, trying various experiments, traces, everything I knew. I was stumped. Finally, at about three in the morning, I decided that I was too tired to continue and went home to sleep.

I had a dream that night about balls and sticks moving around, connecting and disconnecting. It was very graceful and seemed familiar. I woke up suddenly and *knew* what my answer was.

The balls were the nodes of the trees, and the sticks were the arcs that held them together. I dialed up, logged on to the timesharing machine, and made one line change. It took about ten minutes to recompile, so I put some music on the stereo, really loud, while I waited. I don't normally listen to loud music but for this moment, it seemed right. By the time the Mahavishnu Orchestra got from "Nothingness" to "Eternity" my compile was complete. I tried it and it worked. I knew it would.

✦

One of the things I really liked doing was mentoring less-experienced programmers. In one case, I was working with an intern I'll call Tom. We had a huge piece of code that needed to run on a brand new platform. I was doing the compiler itself, but Tom was to help me with the rest. There were likely to be all sorts of problems, both with the brand new compiler and with various other things in this huge body of code.

Tom had learned in school about most of the tools we were using, but we had to figure out some of the other tools and the platform itself. It was in many ways very exciting. The first few days, the things that would hold Tom up were trivial.

I'll use the metaphor of a bump in a rug for telling the story. Programmers will see the point, and perhaps non-programmers will get a taste for what it is we do. Somehow, a little wrinkle had happened in the code and Tom tripped over it. In each case I showed him how to solve the problem.

At first, the problems were so trivial that I pretty much led him straight to the obvious solution. Finally, after about five or six of these, he came to me with a problem that was a little harder. This time there was a big fold in the rug, and it was difficult to not trip over it. I used exactly the same technique, but for some reason, now he saw the general approach. When you find a big bump in the rug like this, either you figure out how to pull the rug so that it will lie flat, or you figure out some way of stepping over it reliably without tripping.

From that point on, the problems that Tom brought to me got bigger and bigger, with longer pauses between problems.

Finally, after about three weeks, he came up with a really big one. Some previous programmer, it seems, had cut up a big section of the rug and stapled it to a doorway, completely blocking it. Hmm. This was a strange thing to do. The original programmer must have had a mighty good reason.

So we spent some time investigating. Maybe under some circumstances, that river over there floods and this was a way of keeping the floodwater from coming in. Is that it? Well, it turns out that we now need to get through the doorway, and unstapling the rug each time is not a good solution.

We have several options: we could figure out why the river floods and figure out how to prevent it. Or we could build a dike. Or we could change to using a watertight door that's more attractive and a lot easier to go through than the kludge with the rug. Or maybe it's not even that serious of a problem at all, if it happens rarely enough and the damage is minimal. Maybe we can figure out a way of minimizing the damage on those rare occasions that it does happen.

It's hard to pick from among the options. But the point is that now we have an approach for analyzing and comparing the solutions. The key is learning how to reduce problems to manageable pieces and to trace problems back to their source through careful analysis.

When Tom graduated, he came to work in my group full-time. After a few years of good work, he moved on to another group, and by coincidence his new boss was a friend of mine. When they'd been working together for about a year, my friend said some very nice things about Tom's problem-solving ability, not realizing who his teacher had been. I think it was about a month before I stopped grinning.

Gerhardt

Tall, thin, and pale, with a sharply angular face, he retains his German accent but speaks English very well. To his surprise, he found an American wife (he thought he'd have to go back to Germany to find someone) and now has two towheaded, bilingual kids. Gerhardt throws himself wholeheartedly into new experiences. He brings his international perspective to the issue of why American companies rule the world in software, and he also comments on American culture.

I finished school in Computer Science early, so I thought *ja*, let's make use of that time, and I requested an internship instead of trying to graduate early. I was very interested in how different the culture and the work ethic were, so I thought that seeing the country where computers and software come from would be fun.

I sent résumés to 20 companies, including the big ones like HP, IBM, Microsoft, and Oracle, without even knowing where they were and what they did. One night I got a call from someone at Microsoft, a German guy. "If you can commit to a 12-month project, you can start tomorrow." I called him back the next day and said, "Let's go for it."

I had one week to finish up my thesis, move out of my dorm, store all my things at my parents' home, pick up the visa, get a ticket, and pack my two suitcases. Then I headed off for a country I'd never been in—in fact, I'd never been out of Europe. Within one week I'd found a house to share, and I bought a car for $750. A Honda Civic, ten years old, but it had four wheels and a roof, and it moved. I got a social security card and purchased a bed. That was all I really needed to get started.

My English wasn't very good. After studying in school, I could do okay when reading, and if I prepared myself I could tell you something, but becoming part of a discussion is very difficult to keep up with. By the time you can respond, the topic has already changed. Colloquial language has to be learned on the spot. I learned the hard way that you don't have to answer the question "How do you do?" in great detail.

There are simple things like the strange question you get in restaurants: "Super salad?"

"Sure! Yes, of course!" Then the server and I would stare at each other, not understanding what to say next. You get over this kind of thing pretty quickly, though.

In the International group at Microsoft I really learned what Europe was all about, through meeting people from Belgium, France, Italy, Sweden, Spain. You work together, but in a way that is influenced by your country, your background, and your personality. I'd never encountered that kind of thing in Germany.

Most of those people were bachelors so there was a lot of partying. There was a young culture to get sucked in and just enjoy the heck out of it. And because this was a 12-month stint, I tried to push as much as possible into that little timeframe. Any activity anybody suggested, I jumped in. Everybody was in the same situation, where we thought we'd be there twelve months, or maybe eighteen months.

The first weekend, I went off to Vancouver, Canada, because I thought it was a lifetime opportunity. Then people decided to take a trip to Arizona to look at the Grand Canyon. Suddenly I wasn't in a rush because I applied for a different job in the company, one without a time constraint. I got hooked on the American way of doing business. I decided I was ready to really experience America. I didn't want to hang out with all the Europeans and Latinos anymore. I would get to know those stereotyped Americans. I would sever all my ties to the group I'd been in. I would get to know and appreciate whatever those Americans were doing. That was when the *real* culture shock hit me.

Very quickly I found that it is all very, very shallow. You don't really get to know people. You get the same questions all the time: "Why did you come to the States?" "Isn't it much better here?" And that's about it. You can turn on the tape recorder, almost, to answer the questions. Then the questions turn to the last movie and the last baseball or basketball game.

In Germany discussion is a lot more involved. It's still very stodgy. If you get invited to dinner, that's a serious activity. It takes a long time of getting to know someone to be invited. But even seeing a co-worker in the cafeteria, you debate politics, the general economy. Even things like religion or rich and poor or any of that are pretty casual discussions.

Here, I feel that people avoid the topics so they don't have to maintain a position that might upset some other people, or that someone might disagree with or that's controversial. I had to learn those things.

Also, a lot of people in the group I was trying to get to know had been married right out of college or in college and I felt like the real reason they got married was so they didn't have to go to the movies by themselves. I just didn't fit in. I felt isolated even though I had lots of people around me. I didn't connect with any of them.

I got so frustrated after a half year that I essentially gave up on it. I went back to the diversity of the International folks, and through that I got to know some other Americans who did not fit that stereotype.

I felt more at home and enjoyed it a lot more. The trouble with that was that I hung out with a lot of International people who only came to Microsoft for a year or two and then went back home. So by the time I'd built a relationship—because, again, I'm one of those northern Europeans who take a long time to do such, *ja?*—they left. I wanted to build a family and I wasn't going to be able to accomplish that here. So I decided to leave. I briefly talked to the Microsoft people in Munich, but they only had support and sales functions, which didn't interest me.

Steve Ballmer stopped me in the hall and said, "You know Gerhardt, I heard you are leaving. What's going on? What are you looking for, and how can we keep you?"

I explained that I didn't want to do development anymore; I wanted to see what people were doing with the technology. I'm a people person and I'd rather work with people.

He said, "Microsoft is going to get into the consulting business, working with enterprise customers. Why don't you talk to the person who's in charge of building that group?"

At the time the PCs became serious, not just a glorified typewriter or calculator, Microsoft determined that in order to become an intrinsic part of the IT infrastructure, you had to put some skin [a person] into those companies and say Yes, we're standing behind you. I built a European and American team to do this. I went back to Germany to become part of this operation.

Microsoft was growing like crazy in Europe at this time, the early 90s. I got to know the Peter Principle, where people rise to the level of their incompetence. In a fast-growing organization like this, it was bound to happen: Microsoft was too young to attract senior people and was not willing to pay for senior people. It was deemed that young, enthusiastic people would make up for the incompetence or lack of experience by the effort they'd put in and the enthusiasm they would instill in the organization.

There were people who could handle a project, a single product, for example, very well. They got into marketing and quickly were put in charge of the whole marketing organization. That was okay when it was three people, but it's a whole different ballgame when you have thirty people working for you. That happened all the time; people were totally non-capable of handling the job. The products sold like hotcakes anyway because they were pretty strong.

✦

The European companies had a big disadvantage: the language barrier. Even if there was a local competitor to Microsoft, they could not really turn a profit because their market was too small, and for them to become a big, serious company, they had to invest the money to do the localization, to build the support organization, to build a local infrastructure in each country. And remember that there is no venture capital infrastructure in Europe. So the only choice was get a bank loan, and this was too scary for banks.

So these other companies just couldn't compete, even if they had a superior company. It was left to the American companies to come in and take over Europe for the mass-market applications. If there was a specialized product heavy on service or adaptation, like an SAP, that was okay.

Out of the American companies, Microsoft was the first company to identify that need for localized products and then to build their products in a way that they could be localized. That was a huge advantage over the Lotus, etc. of the time. The marketing of these products could fail and the products would still sell. In a broader sense, it's why American software now is ruling the world.

Some other companies made mistakes in which horse to bet on. Remember, that was the day when Microsoft was second in every category. One by one, every single competitor who was first made a mistake, and in this way presented an opening for Microsoft.

Lotus, for example, bet on OS/2. They were convinced by IBM that Windows was a fad and that OS/2 was going to take over. Lotus owned the spreadsheet space with 1-2-3 on DOS. IBM convinced them that they should go straight to OS/2 to leapfrog over the competition, who was wasting their time writing software to run on Windows. This way they would be writing for next-generation, rather than current technology. Lotus dropped activities on DOS to concentrate 80% on OS/2. When OS/2 didn't take off, they were left behind.

Saying that Microsoft only grew through acquisition of technology and didn't invent anything itself is so much BS because really, when you think about it, none of the technologies were about a great idea. What's far more important is flawless implementation. It's nice to have a wonderful idea, but look at Xerox and how far that carried them. [Xerox PARC pulled together a team of researchers who had invented the mouse, various aspects of the graphical user interface, and other innovations. The ideas were shown to companies including Apple, Microsoft, Sun Microsystems, and IBM. Apple later sued Microsoft for "copying" Apple's graphical user interface, the concept that Xerox's team had pioneered. Apple and Microsoft both made a bit of money off the concept, while Xerox's products never went anywhere.]

It's all about execution. It's not about having a breakthrough technology, it's about using technology to make something easier. And that's about execution, it's not about a great idea.

Microsoft didn't invent the spreadsheet. VisiCalc is probably closest to that claim to fame, but who knows that name these days? The difference is that Microsoft managed to improve on that concept over and over again with an amazing amount of persistence and attention to detail.

They constantly went back to the customer and said, "What will it take for you to use this product rather than that one?" How can you improve the heck out of it so that the masses can use it? And that's not about a breakthrough idea. It requires a lot of listening and a lot of persistence.

Microsoft had the financial freedom to do what was believed to be the good thing to do, even if it didn't work the first time. Bill's contribution was to see that vision and to see it through, to make the tough decisions. Sometimes it is actually better to acknowledge that something isn't going to work and to dump that effort. Or to see that this might not work right now, but if we do this or that, we can make it work.

Bill has several times said "Yes, I did make a mistake when I didn't acquire Novell, I did make a mistake when I ignored the Internet." He has no problem with that.

Just compare Microsoft with any of the big companies, like an IBM, DEC, Xerox. They have not been able to reinvent themselves so completely. Microsoft has over and over proven that it can reinvent itself. That is truly amazing to me. It's stunning, that continuous basis to restructure the company, to realign responsibilities. How often has Steve's role changed over the years?

MS is totally paranoid, which is wonderful. MS is constantly thinking *What's it going to take to make a customer happy?* and therefore succeed in the marketplace.

This single platform, Windows, has advanced the industry so much it's unbelievable. Yes, it is scary that the platform is owned by one company. But if Microsoft screws that platform up, it will be a thing of yesterday very quickly. There are enough other entities out there that are constantly challenging us...the Internet is changing so many variables. If Microsoft doesn't continue to innovate, Linux will take over overnight. If Microsoft raises prices to where it becomes a problem, Linux will take over.

Can you even have distributed ownership of a standard platform? The Internet has allowed people to collaborate in a lot more efficient way. If you look, for example, at the XML activities, it's quite amazing what type of innovation has happened in that space in very little time.

✦

At some point it got difficult for me to advance at Microsoft. I wanted to advance to the next level, but any manager I interviewed with just looked at my last job and not the breadth of the experience I had gained in various roles. So when an old friend who had previously left MSFT asked me to join a startup and head up its engineering activities, I jumped on that opportunity!

Now I was able to put all my experience together in one role. Soon I became their CTO overseeing all the engineering, documentation, and QA functions. At the same time I also gained great insight into other functions within the startup, such as customer service, marketing, business development, and IT operations. I enjoyed that very much as it was totally new to me and broadened my horizon even further.

Yoshi

Dark haired, brown eyed Yoshi is pragmatic, decisive, blunt, and he expresses his opinions strongly. He deliberately chose to come to Microsoft, unusual in this batch of stories where most of us came by chance or for the job, and not for the company itself. He's tall and slouches casually while he talks quickly and reveals the intensity under the surface. He has quite a bit to say about how people view money, and he challenges those who retire to not merely quit working, but to live authentically.

I was working hard at Adobe in California, in their Quality Assurance department. One day I was about to make a phone call and sell about half of my holdings from the ESPP (employee stock purchase plan), which by the way was better than the option package, when we heard an announcement of a company meeting. So we all filed in to hear Warnock and Geschke speak. Basically they said we were not going to make our numbers and we could not sell stock for three days.

Great. This cut Adobe stock in half. A few days later, at the Seybold conference, Bill Gates got up and said Microsoft was going to make this thing called TrueType (a competitor to Adobe). Adobe stock got cut in half again.

So there I was. I went home and decided that if Bill could get up on stage and say, "We are going to compete," and destroy my financial future, I should work for him. I started planning my departure.

I figured that if I took a project at Adobe that was directly relevant to MS, I would have a good chance of landing a job. So I did that, and we subscribed to the *Seattle Times* Sunday edition to start scoping out places to live. We lived in a condo in Mountain View and for the same price we could buy a home in Woodinville, Washington. With a two-year-old daughter, I felt compelled to own a house with a yard. I read everything I could about MS, and found out that new developers were getting grants of 3,000 shares.

I still recall the night before I went to interview. I always spend some time being conscious of what I am doing and what I am about to do. I visualize the moment. I thought if I could get 300 shares, that would be great. So I decided to ask for 3,000.

The interview day was a long and, as it turned out, a very good day. It went from 7:30 in the morning to about 6:00 that night. I had three "as appropriate" interviews (you only talk to those people if earlier interviews say you're worth seeing) and had an offer to come back for more interviews. I said no thanks to more interviews and let them know my compensation expectation.

I went back to the housing across the street from campus and ran into two guys who also interviewed that day. They said, "Are you just getting done? We were done at 1:00." I thought Hmm, looks good. At that point I knew a job offer was pending, and I went looking for houses the next day. I found a house and made an offer on it that was accepted.

✦

So I am a software mercenary. The old style of work and pensions is extinct. You get compensated if you work hard but it is merely a long contract. I am loyal as long as I am paid for my time and effort. I am a hired gun. I believe there is no dishonor to this view. In fact, I think it is more realistic and closer to how MS thinks of its people.

Yoshi

✦

People tend to be dysfunctional around money. Maybe it goes back to the 60's when it was bad to make money, somehow spiritually corrupt. As a result, people tend to be neurotic about money and unable to think clearly about it. I tell my daughter that money has been around for thousands of years. You don't chase or bow down to money, but you don't ignore it or be stupid with it. It is an integral part of life, so get proficient with handling it and get familiar with your feelings about it. Anything less is a copout.

I don't think people have a clue when they say, "If I made a million bucks I would…" First off, a million dollars is *not* enough to retire if you are under 50 years old. Second, 42% of that would be lost to taxes. So what would one do with 580K? Most people don't have any idea, because they have never gone through what it takes to make that much money. It would be like a recreational athlete saying how they would feel winning a professional championship. They don't know what it takes to do it, so they have no basis for knowing how it really would feel.

Most people are extremely myopic about money. They can't discern how to handle money when it comes to large amounts. People begin by dealing in increments of $10 and $100, then they learn $1,000s and someday $10,000 when they own a house. But that is about it.

If they think you have larger amounts of money, they project their myopia upon you. They believe that if you have hundreds of thousands or millions of dollars, then somehow the rules of managing tens, hundreds, and thousands of dollars don't apply. They would think it silly for you to want a use $1-off coupon on a $3 purchase. Or for you to not shop around for new auto tires and save, say, $100.

Here's another example. You are at dinner. It comes up in conversation that you just bought a second home. To you, that is an investment because it represents, say, 10% of your portfolio. The group decides to order some wine, a Chianti. Do you order the $30 bottle or the $100 bottle? You order the $30 bottle because it is a Chianti and that should be plenty to get a great bottle. You spend $30 because it is the best *value*. On the other side of the table, they think you should buy the $100 bottle. Why? Because you just bought a vacation house. They figure if you can spend that much money, what's an extra $70 on wine? They can't distinguish between the value of a 500K investment and an extra $70 on a bottle of wine, or roughly 200% more.

You get this all the time. People think that because you have millions, that twenty or fifty bucks should be nothing. It is also part of the mentality of "getting a Microsoft millionaire to fund us on a $100,000 venture."

This goes back to going through what it takes to make millions. I did everything I could to save my stock options. I didn't sell a single share for seven years. I scrimped, saved, and used coupons and value days for those seven years. I drank water when I went out to lunch, not soda, because the drink increases a $5 lunch to a $6 lunch—or 20%— and soda is junk to begin with. Yeah, I am hardcore, but I also was a millionaire by 30 and retired before 35.

There are a lot of people who can't make the adjustment. Can't see the difference between the zeros.

Another great one is borrowing money. People think that you should give them money, or at least lend it to them. I get it often. Someone has not planned well enough and comes running to me at the last minute to bail them out. Often they've been reckless and irresponsible in their financial dealings. They figure you can help them and that it won't matter to you. These people are the *worst* ones to loan money to because they simply can't handle their money. If they could, they would not be coming to you.

Good rule of thumb: if someone asks for money, ask them for their complete financial history, as a bank would. Ask them to wait 90 days before you even give them an answer. Only loan them money at what a bank would, plus 5%. And loan half as much as a bank would. If they balk, tell them you don't have 23 billion dollars like Bank of

America or Wells Fargo. If they give some BS about being a friend, explain to them that they are either using their friendship as collateral or are not really a friend because a friend would not put another in such a position.

✦

Retirement removes distractions. You no longer have to spend two hours driving, eight to ten hours working, and two hours decompressing. When you're working, most, if not all, of your time is spoken for by other people's needs. All that changes. It reminds me of the question you get when you are a kid, "What are you going to be when you grow up?" That question resurfaces.

However, it is a bit deeper than it looks. The obvious reply goes, "I am going to do XYZ." But how different is that from what you were doing before? If you do it the same way, with the same pressure-cooker methods, and same mental attitude, it is not really that different. The venue changes but the beat of the music remains the same.

A more interesting question is how will you do things differently? That is where the real exploration begins. Can you be another type of person with a different type of attitude? Are you brave enough to step out of your old ways to explore a change of demeanor? Can you achieve a new level of comfort with yourself?

It is all too easy to be the same person, just doing different things. It might turn out that changing the way you do things is more rewarding than changing what you do. Your demeanor is more a part of you than any task, job, or hobby.

Most people never even consider this type of change unless a life-threatening event occurs. It is optional, but early retirement makes it possible. It also explains why so many people can't make the adjustment. They might not be working at MSFT, but they are still in a rut.

Ben

He's a friendly, open guy with a relaxed style who smiles easily. His long dark hair and pierced ear reveal him for the musician he is. Ben is a fast, energetic talker and he's been a doer from the time he was a boy, when he always had a money-making venture going. He usually has no fewer than two careers at a time but he never looks rushed. His lack of a college degree didn't slow him down, and he has a story that begins in a mobile home and ends in a helicopter. He's at the controls.

Since leaving Washington's preeminent software company in 1994 after eight enthralling years, it's gotten to the point that I can no longer say The Word. You know the one: the nine-letter word that begins with M and ends with *icrosoft*.

It hasn't always been this way. I've developed alternate ways of talking about anything having to do with the company itself or my employment there. Among my closest friends, a majority of whom once worked there as well, I've come to substitute the term "M-Bop" instead of using The Word. This is particularly important if my friends hope to draw me into conversation about The Topic while in public. That's one of my steadfast rules. Don't use The Word in public.

Having been an employee of M-Bop seems to open doors to certain none-of-your-business questions while also marking you permanently.

Don't get me wrong, the marking can be an advantage. There's no doubt it is of assistance when talking with one's mortgage broker or flavor-of-the-month electronics-toy salesperson, and it definitely looks good on a résumé when job hunting. However, it's an unwanted tattoo when a complete stranger wants something from you—conversationally or financially—because they've heard you once worked for the company that, according to journalistic folklore, turned one in five of its mid- to late-1980s employees into millionaires.

✦

My upbringing was honest and real even if my childhood memories now seem to be from another world. We lived in a single-wide mobile home as the caretaker family of a prune orchard. Dad's blue-collar job with the Oregon State Highway Department put fried chicken and fried potatoes on the dinner table one night, fried pork chops and beans the next.

I devised ways to make money when I was too young for paper routes and lawn-mowing jobs. These schemes ran the gamut from talent shows in my family's two-car garage (we had upgraded to a simple 1950s shoebox-shaped house) to making beaded jewelry on a small loom that my father helped me construct.

By the time I was in junior high school, I was making several hundred dollars a month selling my macramé arrangements at the two local hobby shops and taking custom orders from friends, family members, and clients. Jute, beads, and potted hanging plants were quite the decorating rage in the 1970s, so making macramé arrangements was relatively easy money when I wasn't distracted by my first attempts at girl chasing, my first car, my first electric guitar, or my first stereo.

Being good with my hands and fingers, I was instantly attracted to typing when offered the class as a freshman in high school. I was uninterested in dirty manual labor like the line of work my father had moved into: diesel mechanic.

Late in ninth grade my typing teacher recognized that I was reaching a speed where I could outrun the early IBM Selectrics and most of the manual typewriters available in class. He challenged me to learn to think of words as bursts of letters instead of as single letters. In other words, the word "conscience" was a burst of the word "con" and the word "science." This allowed me to type a three-letter word followed by a seven-letter word, each with a certain associated muscle movement.

This burst approach affected me in other ways that have stayed with me. When a person is talking to me I often know the number of letters in a sentence before I process and deliver a reply. This quirk goes deeper sometimes, causing me to visualize how to type a sentence as someone speaks it, or to count the number of left-hand typewritten letters in their sentence versus right-hand typewritten letters. But that's another story.

✦

Life was moving quickly; I was now 20 years old and married, working full-time. I was convinced that college wasn't in the cards for me. The one term I attended at the local community college got in the way of working at the daily newspaper and rehearsing with my band. Since coming to the conclusion that I didn't need a college education, I've not allowed the lack of a degree to stand in my way.

Then hard times hit. A combination of slowing work and the fact that I failed to recognize that I was being asked to step up to supervisory and trafficking [scheduling and routing] responsibilities at my job resulted in me being laid off.

I was devastated, having never known anyone who had lost a job in this manner. My childhood experience with people losing their jobs always had to do with seasonal and sawmill or timber industry layoffs. Fortunately, I had been hard at work cooking up a publishing venture and this seemed like the time to move forward with my plan.

At the time, there were two different classified advertising tabloids being published in Eugene. The illegibility and non-categorized format I saw with these publications planted a seed in my mind: what if someone published a similar tabloid, but placed each advertisement within a category, just like a daily newspaper?

After several weeks of calculating ad rates, potential costs and income, calling advertisers, and clearing things with my wife, I managed to convince my father to invest $600 in my venture. My *ADventure Classifieds* was only a mild success in the 13 or 14 weekly issues I published before being too strapped to continue.

My wife and I were considering a move from Oregon to San Francisco, so I began reading classifieds from the Bay Area. I found an advertisement for a Composition Supervisor for Microsoft Press running in the *San Francisco Chronicle*. How timely that this Redmond, Washington company was hiring for a position that seemed to be right up my alley. Since I had never heard of the company whose claim to fame at the time was MS-DOS, it seemed, at the least, to be an opportunity to prime myself for finding a job in San Francisco.

The interview process proved to be daunting. Starting with the initial phone interview, things seemed unreal. Never before had a company taken the time to interview me prior to meeting with me.

What I had failed to understand was that M-Bop would be absorbing my expenses to get to Washington State; I had thought it would be my responsibility to pay. When they called a week later offering to fly me to Redmond for an interview, I was dumbfounded. How could a company afford to spend so much on recruitment?

Interviews lasted most of the day. Lunch was spent interviewing on a park bench alongside one of the duck ponds that sit between the original Buildings 1 through 4. M-Bop had not only spent the money to fly me to Seattle, they provided me with a rental car, a room, and meals. After the interviews I went back to my king-sized room and jumped up and down on the beds, bouncing back and forth between the two of them. I couldn't contain myself. Nothing seemed real, especially the attention they were paying me.

Apparently, the recruiter didn't care for me, as was revealed to me some years later by my hiring manager. Was it the way I answered her silly question about telling white lies to my employees? Was it the fake snakeskin briefcase I carried with me to the interview? Was it the ill-fitting suit I had borrowed from a friend in Eugene? Was it the fact that I had the word "green" written all over my face? Whatever it was, I wouldn't receive any kind of communication from M-Bop for over four weeks.

Then the call came. They wanted me to start in a week and they were offering an annual salary of $25,000. Stock options? I'd never heard of such a thing and none were offered. Hell, the salary seemed like an exorbitant amount of money to someone who was only earning $13,000 annually at the time. Additionally, they were offering to pay to fly my wife and me to Seattle to shop for a place to live; to send a moving company to our Eugene duplex to pack everything for us, including our car, and ship it all to our new Washington residence; to fly us and our two dachshunds to Seattle and put us up until our household goods were delivered. I was thoroughly terrified to tell the Human Resources person offering me the job that I was on an annual employment contract with the *Emerald* that required a 30-day notice. What would Microsoft say? When I finally broke this news, they were still willing to wait.

Someone forgot to tell me that the cost of living on the Eastside [communities east of Seattle] would easily eat up the difference between my Eugene wages and my new high-flying salary. Chalk that up to being young and naïve.

So in early 1986, at the age of 23, I started as Supervisor of one department in Microsoft Press. I seem to recall being employee #1047. By the time I left mid-1994, there were three departments answering to me, and over 14,000 other people working for the same cause.

It's a calculated use of the word cause, because in the late 1980s, and with the smaller size of the company, it really did feel like everyone was working for a common cause: "a computer in every home and on every desktop (running Microsoft software)." The blinding effect of stock options weren't fogging everyone's vision just yet.

By the mid-1990s, it was impossible for me to make a final decision for any of my departments without seeking approval from two to three layers of management above me. Microsoft Press had gone from swift and effective to slow, layered, and sunk in the nit-picky pastime of micromanagement.

A great deal of this management layering was due to growth, but an equal amount was due to realignments and power struggles due to distrust. In my opinion, it was mostly my co-workers' distrust of the technology we could have used to do our jobs. It's more than a little ironic.

Microsoft Press's titles were reaching stores weeks after competitors' titles hit the shelves, causing lower sales for our books. Competing publishers were placing their titles on bookstore shelves before software was even released, and despite errors in their books, this was resulting in them taking a larger market share.

During a management retreat in the early 1990s, I pushed for Microsoft Press to redefine quality so that we could get to market earlier. After all, other book publishers were knowingly releasing inferior titles and then making corrections in their reprints. It was my opinion that if Microsoft Press could define quality, assign a number to the definition (Microsoft Press books=100, for instance), and then place this level of quality on a timeline, we could develop a set of processes that would allow us to publish books quicker by allowing ourselves to publish a level-90 quality book that would be to market x weeks quicker.

Part of my hidden agenda for defining quality included a desire to incorporate some of Microsoft Press's routing into electronic passes that would be handled by Editorial *in* Editorial. The closest we would get to this dream before my departure would be on one of the smallest pieces we produced, a Quick Reference Guide for Microsoft Word.

That project was one of the turning points toward what I understand to be a fully-integrated electronic involvement by Editorial currently being used at Microsoft Press. This at least addressed the issue of using technology to speed up the process, even though Press chose not to establish an acceptable-but-not-perfect level of quality in the content.

The longer one lives in the great city of Seattle, the more one senses that everyone in Seattle: 1) has worked for Billg's technological machine; 2) has a relative who has worked there; 3) has a close personal or professional relationship with a current employee there; 4) has interviewed there in the last three months and is on the verge of a stock-rich job offer. It's impossible to escape the daily inundation.

Everyone seems to *know* the latest dirt about one of the greatest corporate things to happen to Washington State. Whether I choose to stand in line at my neighborhood coffeehouse, dine out, or read a local publication, there seems to be an M-angle. Having spent seven-plus years working in daily newspaper production, I came to know that certain stories sell publications.

My particular annoyance is that everyone seems to think they have an insider's point of view of the Eastside's number-one employer. They don't, and they probably never will. It's my opinion that you have to have worked at M-Bop prior to 1990 to have a real understanding of what makes the company tick. And if you've never worked *at* and *for* the company (working as a contractor for another company that sells services to M-Bop, even on-campus, doesn't count), then all of your understanding is based on secondhand information.

I consider myself very lucky in a lot of things. Being lucky, however, carries a burden in my life as well. Personally, I don't think that I'm undeservedly lucky; I believe that what has come into my life has come for a good reason, and because I'm a good person. However, there have been those who have passed through my life who, through jealousy, have tried to pass off my accomplishments as simply me being in the right place at the right time instead of me possessing talent.

Self-doubt has made me feel at times as if my Chinese astrological animal—the Rabbit, which is defined as lucky—is the only reason I've gotten anywhere in life.

The two lines of work I've been involved with since leaving M-Bop are quite different from what I did while employed on the far side of Lake Washington. They're both long-term interests of mine, things that I've been fortunate enough to learn at my own pace, but both of which I probably couldn't have afforded to embark upon without the luck handed to me during my M-Bop tenure. That luck, of course, was stock options.

One of my pursuits, being a technology investor, allows me anonymity. No one needs to know who I am or where I got my money as long as I have the cash when the tax man or broker comes around. This line of work fills my desire to keep a finger on the pulse of technology. I can use what I know about where the technology comes from and where I think it's going. It also feeds my need for high-stress-level risk management. While working in the X-shaped buildings, I often put off certain tasks, like the writing of biannual employee reviews, until the last 48 hours of the deadline. For me, this allowed a focus much like sitting in a silent tunnel wherein my productivity was raised to an absurdly high level, one that I couldn't sustain endlessly.

The second pursuit speaks much more to my passionate side, and is so distant from my previous career that no one needs to know about my previous life. There are two things that make my heart sing: one is climbing onto a stage with a guitar strapped around my neck and a cold beer in my hand; the other is flying a jet-turbine helicopter in challenging and difficult situations. Prior to leaving M-Bop, I had nearly completed the training necessary to receive my private license to fly helicopters. Within three months of leaving, I formed Cowboy Copters, which eventually became a flight school.

By midwinter of 1997, I was distraught by the amount of my own cash that I continually had to dump into Cowboy Copters to keep it afloat. I was also distressed by the amount of liability I carried despite having as much insurance as was fiscally responsible for the operation of a flight school. When you own a flight school, it's not a case of *if* a crash will eventually take place, it's a case of *when*, and this fact was wearing on my emotions since I had worked so hard to build the business to its current level. I knew that one fatal crash and a lost lawsuit could mean the end of the company and my financial security.

In the spring of 1998 I was hired by a helicopter tour operator in Alaska. While working there from May through October, I had the pleasure of flying both the Eurocopter Aerospatiale AS-350BA and AS-350B2 loaded with tourists anxious to see the Mendenhall Glacier and the surrounding Juneau ice field.

In addition, I continued to manage Cowboy Copters long-distance. Eventually I sold the company. All in all, there were more than six figures' worth of money that I never recovered in the sale price. But I've no regrets. How else could I have ever obtained the experience I gained, or the name it made for me in the industry?

With Cowboy Copters no longer a burden, I returned to the tour operator in Juneau only to be assigned to two more types of helicopters: the McDonnell-Douglas MD-500D and the Eurocopter EC-120B. And instead of being mostly assigned to tours, in my second season I acted as the Forest Service contract pilot and company charter pilot. This type of flying took me all over southeast Alaska, from Skagway to Haines to Sitka to Petersburg and Wrangell. Forest Service work included doing plant inventories, animal surveys, fish counting, and timber cruising. When not flying in the bush, and while in Juneau, I'd perform fill-in duties as a tour pilot, which seemed rather dull compared to flying out in nature with a loaded gun on the seat next to me.

My third season in Alaska, there were more bear sightings and encounters than the previous two summers combined. Why so many more bears? If you don't think overfishing in the lower 48 is affecting habitat up north, go to Alaska and see how it has decimated the fish runs, and how this is cutting into the amount of fish available for the bears and the wolves and the eagles. If that doesn't interest you, you're probably not interested in the accelerated disappearance of the glaciers and ice fields either. But that's another topic altogether.

Within this Alaskan company, there are a few close friends who know of my past. But to the rest of the employees, I'm just one of fifteen helicopter pilots working for a company that makes the majority of its money from cruise ship tourism in southeast Alaska. I like it that way.

Carlos

Carlos is a tall, dark-haired man who speaks readily and warmly of work and his family. If you meet him once, he'll remember you. He's easy to talk with—words are his business, as a reporter, tech writer, and now a high-octane marketer. Not many people can pull off that kind of career path and do as well as he's done at each job; he has the innate talent and puts in the effort to succeed. He's a close observer of people and events and is grateful for his time at Microsoft.

I could write a book on each of my parents, an unlikely mix of a second-generation Mexican dad from Texas and a thoroughly Anglo mom from Ohio. Dad was among the first group of four Mexicans who marched with the cadets at Texas A&M. After having four kids, for a variety of reasons—not the least of which was stark poverty—they split up on amiable terms. He left when I was about six months old.

The four of us were raised near Cleveland by my incredible, resourceful, tough-as-nails mom. Ultimately it gave us a strong work ethic, a bond with each other, and a sense of what matters in life. We moved around a lot, staying one step ahead of the bill collectors. Mom taught herself how to program mainframe computers and had to make her way as one of the first women programmers.

She lived her life with an incredible authenticity and suffered for that. Her approach taught me that I could be in possession of my own life; no one would have to tell me what it would be. She gave me a sense of possibility and I started having great adventures very early.

I grew up understanding what a gift and a blessing it is to have the opportunity to work. It was a great goal in life to have a job; having a job you loved was beyond my comprehension. I started working when I was 10, with a paper route. When I was 13, I realized that if I did well in school, I'd probably be able to get into a good college, and that would be my way out of our hand-to-mouth existence. I was determined not to suffer like my mother did. She paid a high price in stress to be a single mother in the 1960s and she died young.

I went to Alaska during high school summers and then moved there after college. It was an unusual move for a kid from Ohio, but I fell in love with Alaska, where I began a career in journalism that lasted seven years. It's a pretty rotten career, though. It's tough to get to the top of the heap in journalism.

I had a sudden opportunity to go to Washington and work for NPR, National Public Radio. I turned it down because I couldn't break the deep connections I had with Alaska as abruptly as they wanted me to.

When I was 30, I drove to Seattle with everything I owned in the back of a Toyota pickup truck. I had no prospects and I slept on the floor at the house of the one guy I knew in town. I eventually got a reporting job at the *Seattle Times*. Along the way, I did some technical writing to pay the bills. It was an easy way to make money, but not something I particularly enjoyed.

Then I met a woman who did contract [on a contract, not full-time] writing for Microsoft and she talked the place up. With some minor trepidation, I checked it out and was offered contract writing work at $20 an hour, a huge amount of money for me.

But I really didn't come to Microsoft for the money, because I'd pretty well carved out a way of operating in the world that was independent of money past a certain minimal point. I knew how to get by on very little and I knew that happiness is unconnected to money. If you have an absolute lack of money, you can't be happy, but really, you don't need much of an income to be happy. It's not connected to what makes the soul happy. That's easy to forget in an environment where people are as blessed as they are at Microsoft.

I became energized at Microsoft because it had *winner* written all over it in 1988. It wasn't in an in-your-face way, or an arrogant way; I was stunned to see all these people wearing normal clothes, with this incredible unpretentiousness, but who also had this great confidence that collectively they could succeed.

The company made an investment in people, making sure they had what they needed. When I worked at the *Seattle Times*, we used to wait for shipments of pens to arrive and we'd race to the little supply closet. We'd all grab pens and hoard them. My first week at Microsoft, I found the supply room that was loaded with this absolute wealth of supplies. I asked my manager if I could have some of these things, and of course I could, that's what they were for. I took a brown paper bag and loaded up. For a year, as I moved from office to office, I had this bag that I would dip into when I needed something. I eventually realized that the office supplies were going to be there tomorrow, so I took my bag to the supply room and put things back.

At other workplaces, you come to understand that situations can play out in any of a multitude of ways. At Microsoft, there are really only two alternatives: we either succeed or we fail. And we take the lessons from failure so we can succeed next time. Nobody even gets into the tent who doesn't have this essential optimism. I remember thinking Please, God, let me continue to stay here. I quickly forgot that the rest of the world wasn't like that. That hasn't changed in the thirteen years I've been here.

I've had an unusual career path, starting as a technical writer, then doing instructional design work, then going to work as the editor of the internal newsletter, which I was able to treat as a small newspaper.

I had a lot of experience doing community journalism in Hayes,

Alaska. Some of the oil money flowing through the state was used to put radio stations everywhere, including the 200-person town of Hayes. I became the news guy, and of my own volition, I ran local news twice a day, which was ridiculously ambitious. I used the same idea to create a Microsoft community: pictures, stories, and letters to the editor. Editing the MicroNews got me into a number of places I wouldn't have gone otherwise.

A few years ago Connie Chung visited Microsoft for a segment of Face to Face. She was here—her makeup immaculate and her fangs well hidden—to talk to Bill Gates and I was called, quite unexpectedly, to tag along, take some pictures, and maybe write a story for the newsletter. The only thing I was worried about was how my wife would react when I told her how I'd spent my afternoon on the one day in weeks that she didn't dress me up nicely.

Bill was slated to show off a working prototype of an interactive TV application. This was to be an impressive tour de force of advanced technology that would instill in Connie an awed respect for Microsoft's prowess in laying out the foundations for the big data turnpike. Little did any of us suspect how bumpy the road would be.

The thing started well enough. Bill was holding what looked like your basic VCR remote control, and he clicked it toward a small black box that was sitting next to a TV. Every time one of Bill's commands registered, the box played a little Ding! just like the right-answer noise on Jeopardy. Then the TV moved on to some new and interesting screen.

Slowly and uncomfortably, it became evident that something was going wrong. Bill was getting frustrated with the black box before him and his narrative began to disintegrate. Bill would push a button and nothing would happen. Then, moments later and with no provocation: Ding! The tollbooth of tomorrow, like most prototype systems, was just plain slow. Increasingly frustrated by the recalcitrant remote control, Bill started pushing buttons like a kid upset with a video game. Everyone in the room fell silent, except for Connie, who occasionally made blithe comments like "This is like me trying to program my VCR!"

Painfully, Bill fumbled to a conclusion of the demo with some help along the way from an agonized young Microsoft technician. The CBS people, seasoned pros who'd seen more than their share of disasters, kept their eyes down and quietly began to gather their equipment.

Just as they passed close to Connie, she cheerfully stopped them.

"Oh, I have just one more question," she said to Bill with a bright smile. She turned to the camera people and said, "Can you guys just set up here?"

The cameras dropped directly beside Bill, in tight for that nice close-up. The cameras started rolling again, and Connie folded her arms. She turned to Bill, her face businesslike.

"Now Bill," she said. "How does it make you feel when one of your most important technology demonstrations just fails like that?"

Bill began to blurt out some kind of an answer, but it wasn't over. "Is someone going to get fired for this?" Connie asked, looking very concerned. "Are heads going to roll?"

Bill stammered out an answer about new technology and the notorious instability of prototypes, and as he spoke, he managed to gather himself, finishing finally with a weak smile and the conclusion that, "It's just bad luck." Which was, in typical Bill fashion, essentially the truth.

Another appointment called me, and I had to leave. I wasn't on hand later in the day when Connie crossed the line with both feet and asked Bill one too many questions that she was asked not to ask. A friend in PR told me that Bill simply stood up and walked away from the interview, never looking back.

No one ever told me officially what happened, but it was made clear to me that no photographs of Connie and Bill, nor any mention whatsoever of the CBS presence on the Microsoft campus that day would be published in my newsletter. The whole experience reminded me of how glad I am to be out of commercial journalism, with its dirty setups. I found myself feeling insulted by Chung's presumptuousness, that she thought she was actually doing serious journalism by embarrassing this guy who, love him or hate him, is one of the great men of our time.

✦

Working for the MicroNews was a stupid career move, although it was fun and interesting. I went from being on product teams to being in a cost center that ended up subsumed in the backwaters of Human Resources, a group about which I have nothing good to say. I had nothing in common with the people I reported to, who saw no value in what I was doing. I got past that job, though, got rid of my leper status, and contemplated what to do next.

I'd always wanted to try marketing or public relations, especially here at this amazing marketing company, but I had no marketing training or background. I thought I had the ability to do it; I just lacked the training. I cast out a couple lines and quickly got connected to a guy who was building a new team to market e-books. He wanted to build a real marketing group. He needed somebody who was a writer and had good communication instincts. We hit it off and he hired me, and within a couple months he'd expanded my duties. I've always loved books and I've always loved publishing. The fact that I get to swim in these waters is a huge side benefit to the job. At some level there's a sense of destiny that it has all come together.

My title now is Group Product Manager. I oversee all of our PR, Web, and communications activities. It's been incredibly difficult to survive; it's at the far edge of my abilities for these past months. I learned a whole new skill, a whole new industry. I travel to some incredible places and rub elbows with incredible people. It's been an exhilarating high-wire existence.

We have a relationship with the *New Yorker*, a magazine I've loved for years. It's a unique presence on the cultural landscape. I was able to attend a session they put on in midtown Manhattan about e-books called Download or Die. A panel of major publishers, a professor emeritus of Yale, and a roomful of dignitaries—and my colleague and

I got to rub elbows with everybody. As I got introduced around as one of the men from Microsoft, it was very interesting to see how people responded to that. There's an immediate respect and sense of curiosity and powerful interest in things Microsoft.

It's funny how different it looks from the inside versus what you might surmise from reading the press. One of the conversations was with Ken Auletta, a reporter who's covered the Microsoft trial. We had a great chat. Here's a journalist who's done a very good job. Journalists aren't the arbiters of truth or fairness; they provide information that helps form the big picture. In the grand scheme of things, journalists have done a lot more to benefit Microsoft than they have to hurt the company.

I found myself talking with the author Salman Rushdie and the Vice President of my group at Microsoft. Salman Rushdie was quite interested in e-books and agreed to come out to Microsoft for a visit.

When we took our VP to the train station that night, he said, "Thanks for making me look good. I recognize that you're the ones doing all the work. You're the ones making it happen." And he told us to go out and have a great dinner on him. We went to a nice restaurant and lifted a glass of good wine to our day: "Just when you think your job can't get any cooler…it gets cooler." I've had about a dozen of these experiences in the past year.

The company has constantly given me new opportunities. To the extent that you have the audacity and the wherewithal to capitalize on them, the company will always open up more opportunities to you. If you're willing to give it more, it will take you higher. I still feel like the sky's the limit.

I'm now at the point where I worry about balance; I worry about whether I'm giving enough to my wife and two sons, paying enough attention to my health and to other interests.

✦

It's funny to watch the company's antitrust tribulations, because my sense is that the company's always been very humble, and that the people inside are very cognizant of how fortunate they are and how they're lucky that they were ready when opportunities appeared. That's why there's this underlying current of constant paranoia—people do realize that we've been very fortunate. We didn't steal this, it wasn't a scam, nothing illegal went on here. It was just a lot of hard work and a big dose of good luck.

There's been a lot of dedication to things that make a company work well, like making sure you hire good people, and making sure you take care of them. When that changes, that's when I'll leave. The evidence that I'm getting now is that Microsoft continues to make the right decisions and the right investments, and they treat people properly.

Ever since I got here, I've felt that Microsoft really challenges you, whether you realize it or not, to be on honest terms with yourself. You really have to know what your life is about and what you're here for. If you have that, you can pretty well endure things. You're constantly in the presence of people who are much better than you in any professional accounting. Maybe Bill Gates and a couple other people aren't confronted with people who are vastly better than they are, but I'd say that even they are humbled by the people around them.

There are constant temptations to measure yourself and to feel bad about yourself. We're all really competitive. You have to be very grounded and have a strong sense of self. The secret to survival is to know who you are and why you're here. And that's asking a lot. Many people don't have that. I'm not saying I have this in spades; there are many days I go home and say, "Wow, I'm an idiot."

✦

Microsoft's never been about money for me. I've always felt like my salary is really good, and given that alone, I'd be fine. I've never gotten the big grants. I was never in a "money" job. It's taken me a long time to become aware of what I've got in the stock options. It's given me this incredible safety net. The money hasn't given me the ability to do whatever I want with my life; I've always felt that I had choices.

A company primarily based on meritocracy thrives over the long term. Microsoft exerts a really powerful gravity about how to succeed. Its definition of success is about teams and products succeeding in the marketplace. It's a good gravity, but it's a mistake to allow it to become your own personal gravity; you have to learn how to harness it, when to use it and when to let it go.

One of the reason I've survived a long time is that it's never bothered me to watch people pass me in their careers. I'll look at a guy like my manager, who's so talented and has a stunning capacity for work and knowledge. There's an awful lot that I can learn from a guy like him. And he's smart enough to know that there are a lot of things to learn from people who aren't like him. Then it goes from saying, "This guy's eating my lunch," to "What can I learn from him?" It goes from competition to benefit. But boy, you have to have your feet solidly on the ground about who you are and where you came from.

It's not for everybody, but it's still cool to be here. I just wish I didn't have to sleep at night. I just wish it didn't all go by so fast.

Gina

A petite, green-eyed blonde, if she's not off playing soccer, riding horses, or shooting photos, she's working miracles in her big garden while her two cats roam nearby. She can be very quiet in a group but talks plenty when she wants to, and laughs often. Gina became a braver person at Microsoft, yet there's also frustration. She reveals what it feels like to be left behind when the gravy train pulls away: she was laid off, worked for another tech company, and then came back to Microsoft.

I started at Microsoft in January of 1989 as a contractor and was hired full-time in less than a year. I despised the company I was working for, so I took great pleasure in giving notice. There wasn't anything they could say, even though they didn't want me to quit, because I was going to Microsoft. My boss couldn't be mad. Who could pass up that opportunity?

Coming into a job where everybody was making things up as they went along gave me the chance to reinvent myself. I had a wardrobe of corporate wear: straight skirts, polyester blouses, high heels and nylons, and those very quickly got put into the back of the closet. There was joy in letting go of the façade and just getting to know who I was.

Before, I was known by my title. Everybody understood what a secretary or an administrative assistant was. Merely working at Microsoft became my identity; people weren't too interested in what I did. I worked in localization and nobody knew what it was. Even my parents thought I was a translator. I see friends of my parents now, years later, and they say to me, "Oh, are you still translating?" I just tell them I don't work for the International group anymore.

On my first day I realized I would either sink or swim. In order to swim I would have to break out, be assertive, find out what I needed to know and not be afraid to ask questions. I had to change my whole way of being.

At Microsoft I was responsible for my decisions. I was used to always having someone checking my work, and I was used to an atmosphere where you covered up your mistakes. It's the opposite at Microsoft. If you cover up, somebody is going to find out, and you look unprofessional for not being honest.

That atmosphere was a big growth experience and it was nice to know that I could handle it, because I was successful immediately. You have the freedom to do things the way that you need to get them done, too, which was really refreshing. Microsoft gives you enough rope to hang yourself. You just have to not hang yourself.

One of the most fun parts about working at Microsoft is the fact that it really is like a college campus. Everybody says that when they go visit, but it's significant and it provided an atmosphere to get to know people and find a group of friends you could socialize with, which you don't necessarily find at other companies. It was a good release from all of the stress. Certain connections came out of that, a tight social network. If a group is technically good but they're not talking to each other, you're not getting the same product that you would otherwise.

You knew you could truly count on these people, especially in International. I can still contact people from the old group, and the network is there. You can ask for favors and you might not have talked for a year and a half, but old co-workers are completely willing to help you. Now groups don't have that connection, except for a few people.

It seems like more and more I hear stories of bad management, where people are stuck in jobs they don't like, where their manager doesn't like them, and they try to leave and they can't. They end up in these strange situations where they're looking for a way out, and it's unnecessarily hard. Managers put blocks on their leaving, saying "Oh, we need you for the next six months," even though the group isn't doing anything. Nowadays it seems that in every group you work in, you only find one truly good person.

Managers nobody wants to work for have created their own little kingdoms and somehow manage to hang on. I keep seeing more and more people who are poisoning whole areas. People were literally being made sick by a certain manager I had and the people who were able to work under her were not the kind of people you'd want to be around. She had severe prejudices, so you were either completely in and golden, or completely out and worthless.

I learned to be more in the world by being exposed to people who are very passionate about many different interests and causes. I'm much more generous with the money that I give to causes than a lot of people I know, even though it's coming out of my normal-size salary.

That's another thing that I've learned at Microsoft: to try new things and not to worry about what you look like doing it or whether you're successful at it. Just be open.

For example, I went on a cross-country ski trip with my brother, a friend of his I'd met briefly, and other people I didn't know. I'm pretty shy, so being stuck with a whole group of people I'd never met before for an entire weekend was a stretch for me, but it just sounded too fun.

It turned out to be a magical time.

I also navigate for a friend in three-day horse-cart driving events on courses with hazards. You never know what the hazards are going to be made of and you're supposed to go through them as fast as possible. You can get bumped out of the cart or jostled over. I'm responsible for memorizing the course and telling the driver which way to go in a split second. I hold a stopwatch and we have to finish each segment within a window of time. If I screw up we get disqualified.

I've done canoeing. I decided I was going to conquer my fear of downhill skiing and took lessons as an adult. I took a three-day sailing course by myself. I took a rafting trip in Utah.

Before this, my life revolved around easy social things like going out to dinner, seeing movies—not physical challenges or doing things with people I didn't know. Even going to school in France for a year in college didn't break me out of my shyness. It was definitely the growth I experienced at Microsoft that pushed me into these new things.

My group was reorganized so many times that I ended up being a Print Production Specialist, responsible for a lot of dry scheduling and coordination tasks. This was after Microsoft had paid to send me back to school to get my certificate in technical writing and editing. My bosses were good about helping me get experience by loaning me to other groups, but nothing came of it; I couldn't get a job doing editing. It was really strange. Even though we had Microsoft people on the board of the certificate program, nobody seemed to value it. Managers were laying off writers and editors and bringing them back as contractors, so people who had full-time jobs were really holding on to them tightly. I was so frustrated.

Then my manager told me he wasn't going to be able to justify my position at the end of the next fiscal year. I had to decide whether I wanted to wait it out and get my severance, which would have been quite a nice package after years of being a full-time employee, or find a job with another group. No luck; I didn't find a job.

The exit interview was especially frustrating. The HR person explained all of the administrative things, asked questions, took notes. Then she asked, "Why are you leaving Microsoft?" At that point, she placed the pencil on the desk. What was the point of asking the question if she didn't record the answer?

I explained that I was being laid off. That I'd gone back to school and after almost five years of service and an excellent record, no one would hire me. She told me that she had heard the exact same thing the day before; the person had even taken the same certificate program I had. She also admitted that she wanted to go back to school and get her master's degree in an area that really interested her, but was afraid that Microsoft wouldn't hire her in a new capacity. So she decided not to do it.

It was really weird to leave Microsoft. My manager let me leave feeling special and with a lot of dignity. He was one of the good managers and I really appreciated that.

I was immediately hired as a technical writer at a software company I'll call Acme. I packed my office at Microsoft on Saturday and started at Acme on Monday. I hit the ground running.

It was ridiculous that the managers I'd interviewed with at Microsoft had thought a writing job was too difficult for me, in spite of my years of experience at Microsoft and going through the writing program. It had always been a part of the Microsoft culture to take a chance on a person's potential. What a switch that Acme was willing to take more of a risk than Microsoft.

Acme was a very different company than Microsoft. Even though the User Ed group had been doing the same thing for years, they didn't have much of a procedural structure in place. It was hard to figure out who to go to for information. Very little was documented, so you had to hunt up information all the time. I called people at Microsoft all the time to get technical questions answered because I had no idea who to talk to at my new company. I was shocked, after being in

International. You walked in to that group and there was a notebook full of all kinds of detailed instructions for every step of the job.

Acme is very much part of the real world: fun is not tolerated. The company is filled with lots of young married couples with small children, so people had a nine-to-five mentality. The flextime was somewhat flexible, but not like what you'd find at Microsoft. You'd certainly never see people walking around barefoot or enjoying any of the personal freedoms you find at Microsoft. You weren't allowed to play computer games. You could sit in a conference room during lunch and play Hearts with real cards, but you couldn't do it on your computer or you'd be fired.

In some ways the atmosphere was very strange, but it was an honest-people-making-honest-wages kind of company. Nobody was going to get rich, especially since the company never went public as they kept saying they would.

The expectations are different outside of Microsoft, too. I did good work at Acme, but I spent the first couple months doing next to nothing and desperately trying to find work to do. I took every relevant class they offered, I checked books out of their meager library, trying to become familiar with anything that I could, and all that was just fine with management.

Once we finally got started, there was one big crunch during the whole project. At Microsoft we have them repeatedly. The crunch was any day in the life of a Microsoft person and these people thought it was amazingly hard. I felt like I was getting away with something by working at such an easy pace, but it was also good to decompress for a while.

The disadvantage was that it felt second-rate and like I was getting behind in my skills by being there. I thought I would never be able to catch up if I stayed there too long. I only made three lasting friends at that company in two and a half years.

Working at Acme woke me up and reminded me of the real world, where people don't have stock options and portfolios. They're putting money away in their 401(k)s and raising families in modest homes. The expectations about what I should have at a certain age were unique to Microsoft.

Most people don't have large homes when they're single, and they're not driving fancy cars and all of this stuff that we see at Microsoft. Nobody has it at Acme; many have it at Microsoft. It made me realize how lucky I was to have walked away with what I did. It also made me realize I didn't want to stay out in the real world. I wanted to go back.

It can be amazingly difficult to get back in. I began to wonder what the hell was wrong with me. I had been here at Microsoft before and had done well. I knew other employees were not better than I was, because we used to work side by side. The whole thing was a blow to my confidence.

Then, through luck, I found a job doing contract writing at MSNBC. It was nice to be back, even if I wasn't a blue badge at first (the card keys for full-timers were blue), before I got hired full time again.

The feeling I had when I went to Acme was that I'd been kicked out of a club. Leaving Microsoft hurt. This time around at Microsoft, it feels scary. I don't know whether it will work out.

The one thing that I'm banking on is that when my boss was rehired, she had to make a three-year commitment to being there because they didn't want her to decide to go back into retirement. I'm working for *her*. I know that she wants me to succeed.

✦

It's been strange to see people who started at Microsoft when I did who have left with a lot of money. Some have retired or at least have taken a few years off until they decide what they want to do next. And I had to walk away from it. I had three grants vesting when I left, and I'd only been able to touch half of one and a quarter of the second; I hadn't been able to touch the third grant at all. My broker advised me to buy everything I could using a margin loan against the stock I'd accumulated through the employee stock purchase plan. So I did, which was smart.

I have a nice nest egg. I can be comfortable with that, knowing that if something happens I can handle it. But the nest egg is certainly nothing I can retire on and it's nothing I would want to dig into to take a year off to travel.

A single friend had me over to see her house, an older home with great character. She'd decorated every room with coordinated window coverings and bed linens and nice wall colors. She described what she wanted to have done in her yard, and how she was going to pay a landscaper to do it all for her.

I felt like I was being kicked in the stomach. I wanted the freedom to be able to live like that. It shocked me; I'd really felt equal to her until then. We'd both been at Microsoft for a while, we were both single, but the circumstances worked out so differently for us. When it came down to it, she had the money to buy that house and decorate it and to retire.

I have my own house, about the size of a cozy apartment, and it's great to own a home, but it's not decorated and color coordinated. I have to watch my finances, and my money goes into things like water heaters that die.

I also know some people at Microsoft who never got any stock options. I don't talk to them about options; I never mention the word because I know they didn't get them, and I feel bad about it. They still have the employee stock purchase plan and their 401(k)s. I have heard the stories of the people that sold their stock as it vested and they're still working because they blew it all early. That would be maddening to me.

✦

It may not sound like it, but I've gotten past a lot of the bitterness over being let go. Up until recently, it was really hard not to think about how I was forced to walk away from Microsoft.

Why me? Why was I the one to be laid off? What game did I not play right? It's timing—everybody that left International a year before me to take jobs as editors in other groups got hired. It didn't matter if they had the right degrees or any specific training.

I was so close. And I was doing a good job and getting good reviews. I had to leave and then watch a lot of people just put in their time—and they admitted to their friends that they weren't interested in what they were doing. I made the choice to go for the job I wanted instead of just hanging on at Microsoft. Sometimes I really regret my decision. It makes me angry to talk to people that are just vesting. The whole "rest and vest" approach pisses me off—it just doesn't seem honest to me.

I'd like to say to myself that I made the right decision, but there are a lot of fascinating things I'd rather be doing. So what if I'd sold my soul for another five years or so back then?

It feels like I missed the boat. Sometimes I get angry about it. Sometimes I feel betrayed by the company.

I'd like to do things for my family, but I can't. It would be so nice to take care of their needs. If I'd made different decisions, I'd be able to take care of them.

And then I talk to people that don't work at Microsoft and have never worked at Microsoft, and they have absolutely no understanding of any of this. That brings me back to the reality of what I really have, how lucky I am to have it.

I had a chance to pick Door Number Three, with the money for my dreams, and these people didn't even have a chance to pick a door. And yet, to be so close and to make the wrong decision, to pick the wrong door...

✦

I just went to the internal Web site that has my stock options records. I simply wanted to know the price of the grant they gave me when they rehired me. What I found was my complete grant history, even though the former grants aren't mine anymore. I did the math. I would have $2,700,000 today plus whatever would have come from grants offered later.

I cried. I'm still crying. I'm kicking myself for not selling out and trying to find any job just so I could stay and vest. I hate HR for being so callous as to have that information available to me. I want to send them flame mail telling them to erase that data, but at the same time I want it there so I can keep track of just how much I got screwed.

Conrad

What makes this guy stand out? Maybe it's that he's handsome, 6-foot-4 and weightlifter buff, or maybe it's that he's deaf. Many of the deaf give up on living in the hearing world. Not Conrad. And he's a gifted athlete as well as a brainiac—he learned a computer language over a weekend during his interviews at Microsoft. He's well matched by his high-energy wife. We'll get his opinion of Microsoft, how it is to function in the hearing world, and what really matters. Adolescence is tough enough, but it's unimaginable to go to bed a normal kid and wake up in a whole new world. I asked him to tell us about it.

Late one Thursday night when I was 13, I noticed a swelling on either side of my throat. On Friday I had a full-blown case of the mumps. When you're in seventh grade, that's not necessarily bad news—it's a "get out of school free" ticket.

In my case it wasn't just a day to spend sitting in bed, though. I had a science report on the planets of the solar system due the next week. My friend and I were partners for an astronomy project, and he'd picked the stars.

For a hard-core Trekkie this was as much fun as it was work, so I spent most of Friday happily researching and writing. The weekend passed similarly, and by Monday I was over the symptoms of disease. I spent Monday night watching Star Trek and talking on the phone to a friend.

Tuesday morning I was awakened by my alarm clock in a slightly unorthodox way. My stepbrother pushed it in my face, and after a moment I realized it was vibrating but wasn't making any noise. I pushed the switch in and it stopped vibrating. I pulled the switch back out and the vibration recommenced, still without sound. After repeating this a few more times, I looked out of my room to where my stepbrothers were holding their morning jam session and noticed the silence had spread to their electric guitars.

Things really went crazy when I tried to stand up. The inner ear controls the sense of balance and when your hearing is dramatically altered, it affects your ability to do simple things that require balance, like trying to stand up. So I sat back down and waited for the world to stop turning cartwheels around me. The world refused to cooperate.

Then my younger brother came into the room and started to say something. His lips moved but no sound came out. I asked him to say it out loud, and again his lips moved, and again there was no sound. When I informed him of this, he demonstrated that he was indeed making noise by picking up a hammer and slamming it on the top of my desk. Okay, that's pretty hard to fake. Something was definitely amiss. Two weeks later the doctors had given up hope that the hearing loss was temporary.

Summer came and went, and when the next school year began, I traded an English class for a sign language class, picked up a sign language interpreter for my discussion-oriented classes, and remained in the mainstream public school system.

I made it through junior high and high school with a little help from my friends—several teachers, my father, and a couple of classmates who picked up enough signing to keep me in the loop, or at least an approximation of it.

The other thing that helped was that I got into sports. I joined the wrestling team after an unsuccessful attempt at turning my height into an asset for the basketball team. My Dad was happy I was wrestling because it was something he could help me with. He and his best friend Jesse were Bruce Lee's first students, back when Bruce lived in Seattle in the early '60s, and they each taught gung fu to small groups of private students. I trained with Dad and some of that training helped in wrestling.

Following high school, I spent my freshman year at the University of Washington on a one-year National Merit Scholarship, courtesy of a high score on my SATs. When that ran out, I joined my best friend from high school at Washington State University. I left WSU with a B.S. in Computer Science, a letter in wrestling, and a scar on my knee where the doctors fixed a blown ligament after a 300-pound opponent fell on it and ended my senior season.

I wanted to find a job in Seattle, largely to continue working out with my Dad. Unfortunately it didn't look like it was going to work out that way. I managed to get a couple of interviews, and one of them reminded me of a certain fact that was difficult to overlook: being deaf is not exactly beneficial to career development. This interview was for a programming position that fit perfectly with some finance classes I'd taken, and it went beautifully. All the way to the end, where I was told I was one of three candidates for the position. All the way to the point where the interviewer told me he thought I would be the best candidate for the position...*if* I could hear.

These days, with the ADA (Americans with Disabilities Act), that is not something people will say in interviews. They're not even supposed to *think* it. But the position would have placed a heavy premium on communication with external management, and he was conducting the interview by writing on a whiteboard. So it is not difficult to see there would be doubts as to how effectively I could represent the company. Fortunately, things have almost certainly turned out much better than they would have if I'd gotten that job.

Finally, I managed to land a job at a small company named

"Micro…" No, not *that* "Micro…" company, yet. This was Microrim, for Relational Information Management. Microrim developed R:Base, a PC database, which went head-to-head against Ashton-Tate's dBase. We were a close-knit team and many people put in very long hours, myself included. The VP of Development thought it would be good for me to be able to talk back-and-forth with people, and suggested that I get someone who could sign for me. So I called one of my interpreters from high school and she's been with me ever since.

I was also running in local races, lifting weights, and doing gung fu at Dad's, and a year after I blew out my knee, I was playing defensive tackle for a semipro football team and basketball with the Seattle deaf team.

In addition to working and working out, I was dating a bit too. When it comes to being deaf and meeting girls, if you are shy, you might as well forget about it. So I got to be pretty good at starting conversations. The problem, of course, was that after the first couple sentences, we got to the "Well, I'm deaf, do you know how to sign?" part, and things usually went downhill from there. In fact, the friend I'd followed to WSU used to joke that we had the perfect arrangement: I'd start the conversation, then he'd finish it and get the girl. At least, I think he was joking. How do I know what they were saying?

For a while I was going out with a cute, witty, intelligent woman who worked at Microsoft. I'd submitted a résumé to them out of college, but not surprisingly they had not called back. However, I'd picked up the industry attitude on MS, which was that once you signed on, your life was work, minimal sleep, repeat cycle. My friend gently suggested things might not be quite as bad as I thought, but I never really considered it at the time.

Microrim started an ambitious new project after I'd been there for a few years, and beefed up the development staff. Suddenly the money was going out faster than it was coming in. After a "reduction in force," I had to face the sad reality that Microrim was probably not going to make it. Several people I knew had moved to Microsoft. I'd developed a good record of getting things done, particularly in my role on the new project, and I let people know I was looking around. I managed to get an interview for a development position with Microsoft's SQL Server group.

I had very little experience writing directly to the Windows API, and what was this C++ language they were talking about anyway? One of the interviewers suggested that it would be a good thing to know even if I didn't get the job, and as far as I could tell, not getting the job was the likeliest outcome. I spent most of the day being shocked at finding out how little I knew. I had to write several pieces of code, and to this day I think the fact that I misunderstood a question (making it *much* harder) and still came up with a workable answer helped me get the job.

That, and the fact that I had a weekend between the first and second interview days, so I picked up a book on C++ and almost finished it, then had the good luck to run into the same interviewer on the second day and chat knowledgeably on the subject for a few minutes.

The first thing I noticed about Microsoft was that it was like a college campus—in both the tree-lined campus itself, with a fountain and the pond (complete with fish) named Lake Bill, and in how much there was to learn and how there never seemed to be enough time to learn it. I started having a programming book with me wherever I went. Stuck in traffic? Out came Petzold's *Programming Windows*. On the Stairmaster? Don't forget the *Windows Developer Journal*. I hate ads anyway, so I usually have something to read while watching sports on TV. Pretty soon I was fully up to speed and churning out code. As expected, the hours were long, but I had already been putting in a lot of hours at Microrim, so that was not something I was unaccustomed to. But the intensity level was a lot higher—there was always a deadline to meet.

I also had a new athletic goal. I stopped playing football and got back into wrestling, hoping to qualify for the Olympic Trials in Greco-Roman. I spent a couple weeks with the national team at the Olympic Training Center and won the Washington State championships in my weight class (90 kilograms, or 198 pounds). I would run several miles in the morning before work, lift weights at lunchtime, and go to wrestling practice or gung fu in the evenings. Frequently, I would grab some food after practice and head back to the office for more work. I also had a rowing ergometer in my living room, and often would put some time on that late at night while watching a TV show. Closed captioning was catching on, and I was finally able to join the TV generation for more than just sports.

✦

Once I joined Microsoft, I saw that the legends of the Microsoft workweek, although often true, only told part of the story. Yes, the hours can often be intense, and the expectations are high. Yet at the same time, it's exciting because you are doing creative work on something that is going to ship soon, at the forefront of a highly competitive market.

You're always conscious that you are working for a company that is a great success story and that you have a direct role in continuing that success. And, of course, you can see the stock price every day, which helps make the success personal and tangible. Having gone through heavy training as a competitive athlete, I was very familiar with the philosophy that you only get out of things what you put into them, and that to achieve great things, you have to put forth great effort.

Most successful people have accepted that to some extent their lives revolve around their work. That's not to say it's impossible to do a great job without putting in a lot of extra hours. But when you really care about what you're doing, you're not going to cut corners. You're always going to see something more that could be done and the next thing you know, you've signed up to do it, and that time has to come from somewhere.

People at Microsoft are constantly trying to find a better way to do things, to improve their knowledge, to make a new product that fills a new need or opportunity, or to make an existing product better or faster or smaller or more usable. The job becomes internalized into something you really care about. It's not just something that gives you good numbers on your review. It becomes a sense of personal satisfaction when you achieve great results and ship a product that lets people do things they couldn't do before, or helps them do their job better, faster, and more easily.

However, the rest of the world doesn't see all this. They see a big, successful company, and in a competitive world, success for one often means that someone else loses. People love success, unless the other guy is more successful than they are. Then it's human nature to resent it.

So you get competitors, and a few people who think that the spelling "Micro$oft" is the height of wit, pontificating on how evil we are. Unfortunately, a lot of people are willing to listen to them because it's so much more satisfying to believe that anyone who is more successful must have done something wrong to get there than it is to accept that people at Microsoft saw an opportunity, got in the right place at the right time, worked like hell, and made things happen.

A lot of people who buy into the big-is-bad, anti-Microsoft sentiment don't realize how much intensity and effort it takes to put out a large-scale software product that meets a ton of requirements including backwards compatibility (continuing to work with existing applications), new features, speed, reliability, ease of use, documentation, etc., on a tight schedule. Decisions go through a lot of analysis to provide the greatest customer utility while still completing all requirements by the ship date.

As that ship date approaches, the hours and intensity level get turned up several notches. People go into "ship mode," sometimes for months, to make sure all features are complete, everything is tested, all bugs are fixed, and no regressions are introduced. They trade a lot of their personal lives to get a good, solid product out the door.

But, again, our customers don't see this. As long as the product works fine and is easy to use, everything is great. And when customers are happy, they continue merrily along with what they're doing and usually don't make a point of talking about it.

Then they see something they don't understand, or something that doesn't work the way they expect, and understandably become frustrated. Unfortunately, that's when they start talking about the product, or start listening to people who say that Microsoft doesn't care about quality. Nothing could be further from the truth.

✦

Another great benefit of Microsoft for me personally is that computers are ideal for someone who can't hear. Especially now, with email and instant messaging, people outside my group usually don't even know I'm deaf. Writing code is visual, the documentation is visual, and there are many internal email distribution lists for information and peer support.

On the other hand, there are also many situations that require being able to understand what is spoken. Presentations, demos, "brown bags" (lunchtime educational meetings), and the usual meetings with co-workers are all available to me, but they require a sign language interpreter. Microsoft lets me schedule regular hours for my interpreter, so people know when to hold meetings.

I've been with the same interpreter so long that I can read her quite well, but there is a huge amount of mental overhead involved in reading signs and translating them back into the speaker's exact words, and then linking them all together to understand the meaning. Hearing, by contrast, is a much more passive operation.

I saw an article once that said people generally spend about 20% of their conversational effort in actually hearing and understanding what people are saying, and the remaining 80% in thinking about what it means in the context of previous sentences and the subject being discussed and projecting possible implications and responses. I'd say for me those numbers are probably reversed. It is quite exhausting to read signs for a couple of hour-long meetings, and even when I'm fresh it's not nearly as easy as hearing would be.

Microsoft has a very strong focus on workforce diversity and disability accommodation, and nobody at work has ever responded negatively to my deafness. I just tell people I'm deaf and that they'll be talking to me through the interpreter, or maybe writing on the whiteboard or typing into Notepad. It's still quite frustrating to me to have to go through all that, but that's the way it is, and the other people don't have any problem dealing with it.

I have an advantage over many other deaf people in my ability to speak, and I have a lot of practice at guiding the situation in ways that minimize the impact of my being deaf. My work groups have encouraged my interpreter to teach sign language classes, and most of my immediate team members and a number of other co-workers have picked up varying degrees of proficiency.

I don't have an interpreter all of the time, and when I don't, there are some aspects of daily life that it's hard to participate in fully. One example is hallway chats. A lot of conversations, both social and product-oriented, take place on the spur of the moment in the halls or a lounge or a cafeteria. None of my co-workers have developed enough signing ability to interpret at real-time conversational speeds, so I usually can't participate in these without slowing them down. That usually works out okay for simple conversations, but it becomes awkward for complicated discussions.

When you talk to Microsoft people, you hear a lot about how invigorating and energizing it is to be so close to so many smart people. In spite of the best efforts of all involved, there are times that it's just not possible for me to have the same kind of casual, easy interaction that other people do.

Sometimes I just tell people to email me later, or we follow up later when I have an interpreter, so I don't deprive someone else of the opportunity to fully participate in the discussion as they try to translate it for me. I know it's frustrating to them also. Several of them have sent me mail saying how much they wished they could sign more.

✦

My girlfriend and I had been going out since shortly before I joined Microsoft, and after I'd been there a couple years, I asked her to move in with me. She was working hard on her Ph.D. in Industrial Hygiene, so it wasn't really a problem that I was putting in long hours at work.

My Olympic Trials bid had not been successful, and further injury to my knee made it advisable to leave competitive sports, so most of the time I'd spent on sports was put into work. Of course, that time investment was helping me advance. I received good reviews and a couple promotions. And it was great to ship SQL Server and watch it do well, and to see how many people were relying on my components to build their solutions.

Finally, after being together five years, my girlfriend and I went on a vacation to Hawaii and came back married. She chose the specific wedding date because it was the anniversary of the day my stepbrother had put a vibrating but silent alarm clock in my face, and she said she wanted to repair that date. Being a logical engineer, I pointed out that this was quite practical, because if things did not work out, what the hell, that date was already screwed up anyway. As a bit of advice to the reader, I would like to take this opportunity to point out that such observations are not considered romantic.

I bought a motorcycle shortly after the wedding. One of our standing jokes was that she would not let me get one until after we were married, so that she'd get my stock when I wrapped myself around a telephone pole. As autumn progressed it became colder and more difficult to find good riding days. One Saturday in early December, I went out and bought a leather jacket and boots and came home looking like the Terminator.

The next morning I was shaken (battered, even) awake by my excited wife, who was waving a thermometer and pointing at the red line. As I struggled to achieve something approximating consciousness, I realized that it was not exactly a thermometer. Bike leathers one day, first kid the next. This must be in the running for the shortest midlife crisis on record.

My first son was born the following summer and true to form for any new parent, my life would never again be the same. I won't go into detail about the immense feelings of love, caring, protectiveness, and just plain joy that washed over me as I held my firstborn child, because if you've felt them you know what I'm talking about, and if you haven't, there's no way to explain it.

Being a father made it much harder to find the time to put in extended hours at work. I have always felt that being an absentee parent is not acceptable. It's not fair to your spouse or the child, and it really isn't fair to you either. It is incredibly rewarding to bond with your children and watch and help as they grow and learn, developing from squirming bundles of little more than instinctive reflexes to little people with personalities and thoughts and feelings.

However, during my son's first year I was working on a release and it was very difficult to balance the hours at work with time for other things. While I was usually able to get home for dinner, since we lived only a ten-minute bike ride away, I usually had to go back to work afterward and I had to work most weekends. My wife and son went on a trip to visit her parents and I just could not take the time to join them. Thanks to the wonders of email and digital cameras, she was able to send me pictures of him playing in the sun.

Meanwhile, I was just going home long enough to feed the dogs and then returning to work until I was forced to go home for some sleep. The realization that my life had changed and I needed to find a different balance was pounding on the door to my brain, demanding to be let in. Circumstances would soon be handing that realization a sledgehammer.

One of the things I was missing was time with my Dad. I was really looking forward to getting this release out the door so I could get back to seeing him regularly, both for workouts and because I was one of those lucky people who could say my father was one of my best friends.

Unfortunately, despite all his amazing intelligence and knowledge, Dad had one habit that was the absolute height of stupidity. He had been a heavy smoker since age 13, and he had worsening emphysema. I knew my chance to spend time with him was limited and I wanted to make the most of it while I could.

As my work on the release continued through the summer, so did my wife's work on her dissertation. We had planned to have two children and we wanted them close in age so they could grow up doing things together. However, the discovery that she was pregnant again came about three months earlier than we'd planned. Fortunately, she managed to finish and defend her dissertation before the pregnancy became a factor.

She planned a Caribbean cruise for after the release date to celebrate both our accomplishments. As the bug counts declined and the product moved into release-candidate mode, we started getting excited about the trip and I even managed to find time for a clothes-shopping expedition.

Finally, we got the release wrapped up. I made my final fix on Friday the 13th, and we had a very happy dinner as we looked forward to my being able to devote some time to the other important things in my life. We put our son to bed, and as I was getting ready to go to my first workout at Dad's in several months, the phone rang. My brother was calling from the hospital. Dad had been sick with the flu that week, and my brother had gone to check on him and found him having trouble breathing and hardly able to walk. By the time I got to the hospital, he was barely responsive. There might be something to that Friday the 13th thing after all.

Dad never had another workout. He was in the hospital for three weeks, but the outcome was clear well before then. I was with him almost all of the time during the day. Everyone had built up a lot of unused vacation time during the release, so I went on vacation, leaving instructions that I could be paged only if an absolute emergency arose.

My wife offered to cancel the cruise, but there was nothing she could do. I was not going to be much fun to be around even when I was not at the hospital, so I told her to take one of her friends in my place. I went to bed at night with my pager set to vibrate and wrapped to my leg with an ace bandage, in case the hospital called.

We buried Dad a short distance from Bruce, in Seattle's Lake View Cemetery. Like the name says, the lake view is great, and in my mind's eye I can see him signing "beautiful" as he looks out at it. I try to visit whenever something brings me across the lake to Seattle.

✦

Life is too short, and too uncertain, to keep pushing things into the future, to always say, "Someday I'll get to this, but not now." Someday may never come, or it may be too late when it does. Having a family puts a whole new emphasis on the importance of the present. Once you have children, you don't get a chance to be a parent later, when you have more time. If you miss it now, it's gone forever.

It's important to recognize that you can do a great job, and accomplish great things, without feeling obligated to take up every challenge just because it's there. Sometimes it's as simple as deciding what's really important to make the product work, and what's just nice to have, and sometimes the nice-to-have features are worth giving up personal time for and sometimes they aren't. The best time to start making these choices is early in the project.

There will always be situations where things take longer than expected, or something unanticipated occurs, or it's the normal crunch to a release date. You don't always have the option of adjusting the schedule, so you're going to have to invest some personal time to meet your commitments and get the job done.

It can be very hard to find the balance between accomplishing everything you want to at work and preserving your personal time, because when something ships with your name on it, you want it to be perfect. One thing to remember is that no matter how much you finish, there will always be more that could have been done. Features could have been added, or design changes could have been made, if only there had been more time. Work will always be there. There are a lot of other things that won't.

It's a beautiful weekend morning as I write this, and my young son has just come into our home office and climbed into my lap. He wants me to help him assemble some toys he got for his birthday yesterday. It's an easy decision. Monday will be here soon enough. For now, it's time to turn off the computer and focus on another priority.

Ian

Wiry and strong, Ian signed up for a yearlong bike ride around the world at the turn of the millennium. He's quiet, soft-spoken and kind, and when mischief was happening in the early days, like fake memos being put in everyone's mailboxes, he was often a part of it. Ian was the usual bright kid who knew early that he wanted a life in a technical field, even though he was the first in his family to attend college. When he became ill with chronic fatigue syndrome, he found Microsoft's heart.

I'm the eldest of eight kids, some of them step siblings. I was born in Northern Rhodesia, now Zambia, a copper mining town. My parents both worked in the business world, Dad as a management consultant and Mom as an executive secretary and corporate researcher. When politics in Africa got nasty, my parents decided it wasn't a good place for raising kids or having a career. We moved to Germany, England, and then Canada.

I'm the only one who went off to college. My parents were surprised, but I knew by grade 9 that I wanted to study computers. I was always interested in electronics and had my own radio repair shop as a kid.

When I was ready to graduate from the University of Waterloo in 1983, I had 26 interviews with Canadian companies. They'd go great, but then I'd hear that the company couldn't hire anyone due to the recession. One friend took a job at Sears; another took a job with a consulting company that went out of business in two months.

My on-campus interviews with Microsoft went well and they brought me out to Seattle to talk to more people. Steve Ballmer made an offer, and I accepted on the spot. Then I phoned my girlfriend, who said, "You did *what?*" I was in trouble. If I'd told Ballmer I had to think about it, and called my girlfriend first, I don't know what would have happened, but the job had a strong, strong pull. None of my friends had heard of Microsoft and they thought it was a strange choice on my part.

My starting offer was for 2,500 shares of stock and a dog-meat base salary of about $25,000, but compared to other graduates that year in Canada, I was very well paid. A year later, some people were getting offered $30K for the same kind of work.

On my first day, my boss didn't show up because he'd been robbed the night before, confirming all my fears about the U.S. being a scary place. My co-workers sent me into an empty room with something to read, kind of a typical start for a lot of people—no plan or training or anything, just an empty room.

The pressure was intense: at one of the early Friday pizza and beer parties, Bill Gates was chatting with me and he said, "So why isn't Apple MultiPlan [Microsoft's early spreadsheet program for the Apple 3] done yet?" I hadn't even realized that he knew what I was working on, and when the man at the top of the company wants to know why your work isn't done, it's pretty intimidating. Overall, though, I felt excited and happy about the work I did at Microsoft.

As for life outside Microsoft in the early years, we played extremely hard. I put in 120-hour weeks and played on top of that. I eventually cut down to 80-hour weeks and thought I was on vacation. We had spicy foods night, where we'd go out together to eat some kind of hot food, Ethiopian or Mexican or Thai, and cheap movie night. People threw parties all the time, maybe two or three per weekend.

We would talk about Microsoft and about whether the stock would ever be worth anything. Our conclusion was that our stock wouldn't be worth anything because we wouldn't make it as a company. IBM was going to trounce us. We thought we'd survive, but IBM would take over the market. We didn't think of ourselves as a big company, which was one of reasons I wanted to work here.

✦

I was diagnosed with chronic fatigue a few years after joining Microsoft. I was okay in the morning, and then went to lunch and didn't feel so great. An hour later I went home; a couple hours after that I had a temperature of 104. Four days later I went to see a doctor, who went nuts because my liver function was so compromised I was jaundiced and I had classic symptoms of chronic fatigue. It lasted a year and a half.

I took a three-month disability leave, tried to come back to work, and got another 3-month leave. The short-term disability pay was 80 percent of my salary, which didn't cover my mortgage. I was also spending a lot on doctors because insurance covered only 80 percent of my costs. I was tested five times for Epstein-Barr but came up negative each time.

It was extremely stressful to not know what would happen with the disability leave. I was running out of money and was forced to work, in spite of feeling awful and finding it difficult to think. I found out later that some of my friends thought I'd never be back full-time. In fact, some of them drifted away. Others were very supportive and helpful. I was so weak, though, that I didn't have any energy to worry about friends avoiding me.

Then in the end the insurance company disallowed long-term disability. I drained my savings and I had to sell stock to support myself after my short-term disability ran out.

The insurance company's decision meant that I was no longer an employee of Microsoft—yet at the time, Microsoft was still small enough that once you were in, you were really in. You belonged. When I was finally able to work again, I called the manager I'd worked for when I first came to the company, and he was great. He just said, "Okay, we'll find you something."

The illness knocked my career for a loop. While I was gone, there were development lead positions opening up. I could have possibly been in one of those, who knows?

I took the easiest job I could find when I came back, a bottom-level testing job: type this character 255 times and see if the software fails. Type it 256, then 257 times and see if it fails. Testing can be a fun and creative job, but I had to take the worst kind of testing job just so I could be back at work.

I got stronger over time, and could finally start thinking clearly again. I wrote software that automated some of our testing work, and my boss created a development position for me in the test group. I eventually had five developers working for me in the test group, but due to a competing product inside Microsoft, my group got canned. I then moved back into regular development.

When I came to Microsoft, I wanted to do my job better than anyone else. This is being programmed out of me as the years go by. Microsoft does not reward having a less buggy program. They want it out on time, and if it has a few bugs, that's the way it is. I was a lead for a while, but my desire to do things perfectly caused trouble. I'd resist finishing things because they weren't perfect.

Microsoft is teaching me that I need to be less worried over getting things right than getting them done. These days, I don't even worry about performance. I used to code with performance in mind, but now I don't worry about it because of the pressure from management.

Now I'll call a DLL rather than writing the code to provide the specific answer and this library code may do extra work you don't care about. That's inefficient and it bothers me, because I'm a perfectionist.

You can tell that our competitors are in this situation also. We're all on Internet time, where we have to get things out faster than the next guy. It's always been that way for us. Apple is guilty of same things we are. Our products have problems, but our competitors' are way worse.

Some of Apple's features are excellent but their operating system is very buggy: their APIs are so disorganized and poorly put together that I hated working on the Mac, although I liked working on the Apple II. Their operating system also has legacy code as do we, but they aren't doing as good a job at dealing with it. There is a clean, jagged line between the old stuff and the new stuff. Their memory manager is out of the Dark Ages, which is what most developers complain about.

These days we're facing a lot of interconnectivity issues. I'm working on a product with 300 or so pieces that have to work with other products. If you break one piece, it's hard to even figure out which one it was.

Internet Explorer is a good example of interconnectivity: when Internet functionality doesn't work, it really does hurt the operating system, in spite of what the government says. Internet Explorer really can't be pulled out of the operating system without causing major damage. The government is full of hot air on that issue; they don't have a clue.

In the early 80s, a lot of people could say they knew most of what was inside a personal computer. Now there's not a chance that anybody could know even a tenth of what's in there. That's kind of scary. We have to specialize a lot more these days.

One of the things about being at a high tech company for a long time is that you have to get used to learning *all* the time. You can't sit still, you can't say, well, I know what I know and I'll be worth something forever. What you have to learn is hard and there's a lot of it. At least the tools for learning are getting better. The manuals are better, and the online documentation is useful. I used to carry around hundreds of pounds of books because if I needed a certain piece of information, I'd better have that book. Now I carry all those references on one CD-ROM.

If you don't learn enough fast enough, you wash out. You don't have the leisure of a year to get up to speed; you have a matter of weeks or maybe a month. If you don't get up to speed by then, typically you'll hear, "This isn't working, go find a job in another group." If you fail at that, there's a chance you could be fired.

✦

My frustrations with work are reviews and politics, the typical political stuff that happens at many companies. Sometimes I'm told to do something a certain way, even when I know it's wrong. So I do it the wrong way, but in the end it becomes clear that I was right. Then I get penalized, because it's my job to get the code written.

"It wasn't done on time, or done as expected," management says. Their part in insisting I follow a poor design is "irrelevant."

Development isn't asked to participate in the creative planning, and the ideas people come up with aren't doable. We're just told to do things. When we developers protest that something will take three man-years, we're told, "Do it anyway!" We say we won't make the schedule. "Do it anyway!" Then we don't meet the deadline. And it's our fault for not making the schedule.

Bill's influence isn't as strong as it used to be. He still looks over everyone's reviews and changes things like what a feature should do, whether it should be included, and whether features are missing, but he doesn't always get around to this. There just are too many products with too many features for Bill to be on top of everything.

Also, reviews have always been a pain. You work your butt off and get told you did just okay—standards are difficult to apply consistently. You see someone who isn't working as hard as you, but his feature is considered more valuable, so he gets rewarded very well. I've only been that guy once.

When I went and talked to Steve Ballmer about burnout, he told me that nobody was forcing me to work this hard and that I should do what I needed to do. But what he didn't say is that if you don't work hard enough and meet expectations, you'll be canned. It happens frequently.

The bar is always being raised. You can't just continue doing your job. If you do a ton of work, you are expected to keep up that level of production. If I were better at the politics and made more noise about what I accomplish, I'd get ahead faster. I know I'm not assertive enough.

People tell me I'm nuts to stay in my current job, but I love what I'm doing. My managers have told me I make everything look too easy because I do everything I'm supposed to. They tell me it's hard to reward me. What kind of strange logic is this?

I call myself a former potential millionaire. People assume that because I've been a programmer at Microsoft for so long that I'm super rich. I spent my first grant on my car, my house, and surviving while I was sick. I diversified right away, thanks to all the brokers and accountants who told me not to put all my eggs in one basket. I also thought Microsoft wouldn't be worth anything. I have a new strategy: everything you need to do, do it on margin. Don't sell that stock.

After I bought my house and car, I bought other stocks. I have a broker who does most of my thinking for me, which is good because then I can spend my time on work, home, and my wife. Some of these other stocks did okay, but none did as well as Microsoft. I don't like to think much about personal finance because it takes a lot of time to do the research, and it scared me a few times when I let money trickle away by doing what brokers recommended.

My net worth, including the house, is over 1 million. Including my 401(k) it's probably over 2 million. I'll have to work to live, probably, because the bulk of it is in the house and the retirement account.

My siblings have always been happy for me. They didn't realize how much money was involved until five or six years ago, when they saw all the press about Microsoft millionaires. They asked me if I was one of them, but I don't get any hints of weirdness about the money.

My parents are very proud of me. I'm the most successful person in the family, which is kind of weird. They know I work very hard, so they don't resent the windfall.

My family doesn't try to take advantage of me. I've given a few family members some loans—really more like gifts—from time to time. At one point I paid off the house entirely, selling a lot of stock to do so. Then I used a line of equity to loan money to people, so now I have a mortgage again.

✦

I still feel like a kid, enthusiastic for things that interest me, but I'm more centered than when I came to Microsoft. I know my own capabilities better although I'm not always sure other people see that.

I've learned how to learn faster, how to deal with pressure better, to say no, to tell bosses they can't have the code when they want it. I get in less trouble with schedules these days.

My career goes up and down, because you get better at a number of things and you get respected, then you change jobs or the product folds, and you have to prove yourself all over again. What happens a lot these days is technology changes on you, and you suddenly look like a dinosaur and you have to spend a lot of time catching up.

It's always fun working on cutting edge products, and doing things you know other people will see and touch and play with. I am aware that even if I'm never known for it, I've influenced things out there in the world.

Edward

Edward is a slender guy with rock star hair and a bit of swagger. He always has lots of stories about the wild happenings in his life as he pursues his goals. He's both a hyper-logical engineer and a creative, driven musician. He has a big laugh and a beautiful woman on his arm at all times. He talks about the joy of managing projects at Microsoft and the strange twist to his work life: eight projects he worked on were canceled.

I was interested in computers early—I programmed all the attendance and time scheduling for my Canadian high school. The attendance secretary and I had an understanding. She got extra help with the system, and she turned a blind eye to my "mental health" days.

I studied up to the third year of college-level computer science while I was in high school. It was all magical, and I was very drawn to learn more. I'd also been playing keyboards since I was a very young, so beginning early in my life I had two passions: music and computers.

By the time I was ready to head to university, the University of Waterloo's Electrical Engineering program had my name on it. Through the program, I could satisfy my craving for learning down to the electron level what made these machines tick. Through the university's intern program, I spent five years with IBM in Toronto. Again, I gravitated towards all projects based around personal computers and I was first exposed to Microsoft during that time.

When I was ready to graduate in 1987, in one week I interviewed with MS, Northern Telecom, IBM, and Bell Northern Research. The deciding factor in coming to MS was that I felt comfortable and had fun in the interviews.

I was 23 when I started working at Microsoft as a developer on OS/2, and there were 1,500 employees. Initially work felt strange and I was a foreigner in a new land 3,500 miles away from my so-called life.

IBM had been a great place to work, paying time-and-a-half for hours over eight and double-time on Sundays, with food paid for. I had a blast and worked on cool stuff like the PC/AT before it was released to the rest of the world. I made more money (35K) at two-thirds time than in my first year at Microsoft, where I earned 27K.

Right away I worked 12 to 16 hours a day at Microsoft. For the first five years, every three to four months I had a spell of about two months of working seven days a week, 16 hours a day. So everyone was in this mode, there were no meetings, there were no discussions, plus there was the fact that you were supposed to know everything.

It was a bit of a Catch 22 to be so overwhelmed by the work, and yet there wasn't time or a culture that let you be more efficient by sharing information. That's where I think the potential to use people well was lost.

At work, I liked to watch first to figure things out. Things are never the way they're presented initially: you have to figure out what's really important, what the goals are, where things are going, how things get done, what the patterns are. But my first two managers gave me the impression that they thought I was a smart guy and that I should know everything. That made it hard to ask questions or admit being unsure. I think there was a certain amount of macho going on; it was considered wimpy to not do everything on your own.

There was only one culturally accepted way to get the information you needed without looking weak. People working on different projects could talk to each other and share information at company parties and meetings because they were not in your group. When you weren't in a work situation, after a couple beers you could sit down and say you didn't understand something.

The more you talked with others, the more you had the big picture and the easier the job became. Things did get better the higher in the food chain you climbed; either you had the resources to get things done or you could get someone else to solve a problem.

The parties were fun, and they also made work a little less stressful because you didn't have to go through ten hours of trying to sweat something out on your own. Later, when parties got too big to include multiple divisions, the talking stopped.

Two or three weeks after I arrived from Toronto I didn't have anything going on. I just sat on my couch and cried, asking myself what the hell I was doing here. When you're a guy doing this, you feel pretty much like you're hitting rock bottom. Your support network's not there. Your family's not there. You don't have the closeness of a real relationship.

After a few more weeks, I started making friends and finding people to connect with, so I started feeling better. Looking back, there were a number of factors which contributed to my feelings. Culturally, Canadians are much more passive and even though I am not a typical Canadian by any stretch of the imagination, it was still my grounding. There was the loneliness and most of all the fear of failure. I certainly was gonna do what I knew how to do and keep a shiny exterior no matter how uncomfortable I felt, and I was gonna do it alone.

At work there were things that weren't quite as they seemed: OS/ 2 was being positioned as the big rah-rah, but the undercurrents were real and affected the team. We were so far behind the curve, and Ballmer made what became his trademark "We've *got* to make this date come hell or high water" speech. This actually is part of the recipe for today's software production—we just didn't know that we were experiencing a living textbook.

From a statistical point of view Microsoft was very underpowered on the project with IBM. We were responsible for the core OS, and IBM was responsible for Presentation Manager, the windowed API. Our part was first up to bat, was at least 50% of the work, and we did it with about a quarter of the combined work force.

My group was touted as being very important. We were kind of like a SWAT team, coming in and solving each OEM's individual problems. It was funny because my team knew the least of anyone. We had no tools, we had to fight for machines, and we were the last to find things out. The OEMs were using brand new chips that were also unknown so we couldn't tell whether the chip or the software was at fault when our code didn't run. It took an amazing amount of time to do small things.

Our mission was an important one to the success of OS/2 as an OEM vehicle, and properly staffed, properly equipped, and with the luxury of time to allow the various groups to interact, we could have made a much larger impact. There was an obscene amount of work to get done, and since we really couldn't just hire bodies to solve the problem (you had to spend time with each new body), disconnects between reality and what was being said by management created a surreal atmosphere.

After the luster of the cross-border relocation wore off, after hearing for the twentieth time that these deadlines *had* to be met, you knew that the deadline was bullshit, the schedule was bullshit, and the project was bullshit.

✦

My work experience at Microsoft was unusual: 90% of the projects I worked on were eventually canceled, which makes me an expert in the markings of a doomed project. You could just smell them after a while and some of my later projects, especially Talisman, seemed to hire the same group of people as it was exhibiting signs of impending failure. I think of it as the vultures sensing imminent death and showing up to get a good seat.

The roll call of these doomed projects: OS/2, LANMan, WinLogin, Microsoft At Work (which became the prototype for Windows CE), Talisman, Rifff, MSN, and an unnamed, never-heard-from project I called The Return of the Bastard Son of Talisman.

Of course the consequences were threefold: less money for raises, less stock, and less ability to transfer to a great job. Failure was like a giant shitball rolling down the hill. Everyone got covered in it no matter how spectacular your individual performance was. Worst of all, and something I called my last managers on, was that management tried to blame the team for these three consequences, rather than just have the balls to say, "You did a great job, but the higher-ups don't like the project, so we are all gonna swallow this lump of shit because of it."

When it was my turn to explain the retreat of MSN 2.x, I made sure my team of 20 people knew the reality. I took great pride in my work and my team, and when the division got the shaft, I thanked each of them for knocking themselves out. I sent out email to the division head, copying the entire division on it, saying as much. The email had a neutralizing effect on the morale already damaged by failure of the dream and won me huge respect in the halls.

Treating your team with the respect they deserve and being straight with them is the least you can offer as fair barter for their lost weekends and missed family events—not to mention their own lost dreams and missed expectations. For me, this is chapter one in my project development textbook.

Without a doubt the best time for me at Microsoft was when I made the switch from Software Development Engineer to Program Manager. There were two reasons for this. First of all, you have an intricate knowledge of the reality of the trenches and second, it's your job to communicate goals. The feeling of empowerment, of seeing the big picture and having the ability to make sure that each "former you" is properly motivated to get the job done efficiently was incredible. Not only that, but making sure you "managed up" to the Vice Presidents and division heads so that they didn't have an extended stay in the land of delusion was the best antidote to things getting severely out of hand.

I was very successful at this P M thing; things moved very fast for me and promotions came quickly. Within a year and a half I was managing a half-dozen projects and was promoted to Director level.

The in-the-trenches experience of the dark days, the failed projects, the ability to recognize a doomed project, and noting how I felt in all of the situations made a large impact on me. The ability to remember those events and affect new projects positively, and to make sure you earned the respect of your team, are among the most valuable lessons Microsoft taught me.

The greatest single lesson I learned was to never be afraid to ask questions, lots of questions. I questioned the projects I was on, I questioned their schedules, I asked questions as a means to raise visibility, I questioned what made me happy, and where I wanted to take my career. Asking questions makes paths clearer, choices easier, and understanding explicit. It is something I am very comfortable with in technical areas, and something I am applying to the rest of my life.

Microsoft has the potential to change people because of the intense, relentless pressure to do more faster, cheaper, better, and to hit the market hard. Even on the best of days, with the best of teams, this is a tall order.

Starting in Redmond out of university you are overwhelmed by the momentum of projects. You scramble, dash, pump yourself full of caffeine, and *get into it!* You do this again after the project fails, and again after the project changes, and yet again after a major reorg. You keep that energy up, you keep contributing. You are a good Microsoft citizen doing your part for the greater good. You do this for between five and seven years.

One day, however, there's an epiphany. On that day you realize that your lawn is three feet high, you have a stack of unopened bills, and your girlfriend has left you, or worse, found someone else to keep her warm while you slave. Change sets in.

You start to notice that you're more opinionated at group meetings. Schedules, feature sets, and direction are questioned more. A caustic tone creeps into your speech.

More changes set in.

Your patience is a little thinner in other aspects of your life. You see things more clearly now and you're more forceful in doing what is necessary to make plans a reality. You want things to happen faster, cheaper, and more efficiently. You do not have time to waste with people who cannot keep up.

You have been assimilated—resistance was never an issue. You are a member of the collective.

At the end of the Microsoft experience, you will hear from your significant other that you are a demanding person. You will hear from others outside Microsoft that you are opinionated, strong-willed, difficult, and demanding. In every situation you will push others to their extreme, and you will achieve a measure of success.

You will overwhelm most people you come into contact with.

I had a girlfriend in Canada and we were planning to keep up a long distance relationship, but when I got out here, that changed for me. We were so young, and the environment here was so exciting with two or three parties every weekend. There was lots to do here, lots of new experiences to try.

A bunch of us misfits put together a network of unattached, far-from-family people—we were a bunch of geeks who hung out together. I'd go to a bar and chat with someone who looked attractive and I'd get the standard response: "Micro*soft?* Why would anyone call a company *that?*" If you were a guy, you got that from women all the time. So my answer was, "It's Bill's company, not mine! I got hired to help change the image."

In Canada, you pretty much have to lift 600 pounds while twirling a hula hoop on one hand, tell a limerick, and do a quick dance before someone will go out with you. It's a lot of work and women are very fickle. Once you get them, it's great, they're very loyal, but it's a lot of work at first. I was used to having to be charming and witty just to get a woman to go to a movie. When I came down here, I was almost overqualified. I couldn't believe how ridiculously easy it was to get women to go out. Going to bars was like shooting fish in a barrel.

I'm not sure if it's a cultural difference between the States and Canada, but the women here are very confident. Women are much more forward, they ask you out and they let you know they're interested. My Canadian girlfriend was a little quieter, not as outgoing. She came out here for interviews, and I found out afterwards that the paralegal I was dating kept on eye on the process. The paralegal didn't influence the process, but found out that my girlfriend was not getting a job offer. The paralegal told me I didn't need to worry about maintaining a relationship because my life was here, now. It was a new experience to have a woman taking charge, telling me how to live.

The women I met elsewhere, outside of Microsoft, weren't as interesting. Microsoft women have a certain confidence, and there's a certain engaging quality. I lived with one of my Microsoft girlfriends for five years and we were planning to get married. In the end I called it off because I didn't feel that I had experienced enough different people in my life to close that door. It was selfish, but I felt that it was better to be up front about my intentions than end up divorced. Yet I like to have a stable relationship in my life. It frees up part of my brain for my other pursuits when my relationship is taken care of.

I found out there was a group of Microsoft women who shared information about the men they dated. They sent email to each other about where they'd been taken to dinner, was he a big tipper, was he funny, did he spend the night, how was he physically, how deft was he, you name it. They'd actually rate the guys.

I took a woman out to dinner and she said she'd known I was going to do something or another because she'd read about it. I wanted to see the database, but never gained access.

Parties had stopped by the early nineties because Microsoft was so much bigger. Eventually I got tired of the database situation with Microsoft women and didn't date anyone at work for about five years.

✦

Then I met a drop-dead gorgeous blonde at a bar. Her effervescent, charismatic, beautiful, confident, sexual self overwhelmed me. When I went out with her, it fulfilled everything I'd been missing for the last couple of years.

I said to myself Okay, this is a game of chicken. Whatever happens, just go with it. We were each waiting for the other to pull the plug, and neither of us did.

I created a spreadsheet of things I wanted to have resolved before getting married. The list covered things like how the bank accounts would be set up, wills, a prenuptial agreement, and setting a budget. I had a philosophy that if you couldn't talk about these things, why even bother to be married? I knew it wouldn't get easier to talk about things after we were married.

Of course she considered it horrific that I would dare to bring in a *list* when we were talking about *love*...my God. She said that if I truly loved her, we shouldn't need to worry about these things and that she wanted to be with me forever.

Idealistically, yes, it's a wonderful thing, if you could live in that in-love moment for the rest of your life. Now, looking back, I should have made that list twice as long.

She would not agree to having a prenup. Being an engineer, though, I always have a backup plan, and sometimes two levels of backup plans. I talked to a lawyer, who of course suggested a prenup. I told him it couldn't happen—what were my alternatives? He told me about keeping my assets and records separate, how to structure the bank accounts, how to transfer funds when I sold stock, how to convert stock to cash and cash to my accounts so there was no commingling. My wife knew

I was having to do this because she had refused to sign a prenuptial agreement. She probably was hoping I'd screw up on all the careful paperwork, but I never did.

Normally my parents are always there for me. We're an extremely close family, but now they were pulling back from me. I was shocked. My parents are rocks, I couldn't believe they were freaking out. They were reacting to my wife's personality, her being older, her two previous marriages, that she had kids. The night before our wedding, my mom told me I didn't have to do anything I didn't want to do, but people had flown in for the wedding and I felt the pressure of everything people had done for us.

When I woke up on my wedding day, everyone had left the house. I wondered why no one contacted me that morning to hang out with me. It seemed very strange. Where was everyone? Was I supposed to be alone on this day? There was a very weird vibe the whole day; I felt unfocused. I didn't know what else to do, so I went to Tower Records and walked around in a daze. I was thinking that I could just drive away, I could just fly somewhere. I didn't want to get married, but didn't know what to do about it.

There's no script for the guy, no set of things for him to do. My wife had been out on the morning of the wedding getting her hair done and she called me on my cell phone, telling me that I needed to be home right that minute. That was the end of my fantasy about leaving. I was back on the treadmill.

If I could rewrite the script, friends would have been around me that day and we would have talked over a couple of beers at lunch. I would have gotten it out, expressed these feelings, and someone would have helped me see that I didn't have to do this. I'm pretty sure I would have been able to stop things at this point.

I got to the wedding site and slammed about six beers in fifteen minutes. I know what I should have done—just gone up in front of everyone and announced that this was a party, but there would be no wedding. But there was huge pressure to go through with it and I had incredible confidence that I could deal with it.

So, boom, I was married.

Just because you're a millionaire doesn't mean you have to buy everything you want at once. But my wife didn't see it that way. To her, having money meant immediately using it. She wanted to buy a nicer house, buy another car, take her kids on trips, spend ten thousand dollars on a weekend surprise for the kids. I had to sell stock regularly to keep up with the spending.

I had built a professional recording studio in my house. I wrote and recorded music—I play keyboards—with several bands I formed over the years. That was expensive, too.

The music I was working on was under attack; I had to spend my time the way she wanted. I ended up changing my life around so that I could do what I needed at work and not bring it home where she'd interfere or complain. I came home less.

I didn't talk with my friends about what was happening because it was so embarrassing. Everyone had told me not to do this. I felt that it was my problem. I didn't even tell my mom.

I told nobody until about eight months afterwards when I sat down with a friend of mine and had enough to drink that I could get it all out. He suggested that I call my parents, which was great advice. I called and they said that whatever I decided to do, they'd support me. If I decided to get a divorce, they'd support me. My mom told me that I could do anything and not feel bad about it: "If this is what's going on, take steps to protect yourself." Hearing that was the catalyst of change.

I started making decisions for myself and speaking my mind within the relationship. It ended up polarizing the house, with my wife and her kids on one side and me on the other.

After eleven months of marriage, I went on a trip for my music business. My wife had waited for me to go on this trip and her first husband helped her move out. Her kids had been ready to go. She rented another apartment, emptied out the bank account, maxed out the credit cards, and had a lawyer working on everything.

When I came home, it was to an almost empty house. Anything that she wanted was gone. Computers, garbage cans, wastepaper baskets, kitchen things that were mine from years before, afghans from my family, the showerhead. The showerhead!

Even though I had suspected this was coming, it was devastating to come home to that emptiness. The next day, a messenger showed up on my doorstep with divorce papers.

Some of my friends have gone through similar situations with women. I never used to think about the financial aspect of going out with someone. Now I do. Before I offer to pay for things, I think about whether it sets up a precedent for the future—are there ramifications? You think about what the woman's expectations are, why she wants to date. I don't see everything cynically, but you have to be careful, you have to think.

When you need money, it is very comforting to know that it is there. I always called it the money cannon. When you have a problem, pull out the money cannon, aim, and the problem goes away. Without a doubt that creates a feeling of confidence that extends outside Microsoft. Strangely, until you decide to leave Microsoft, it has no effect on your Microsoft life. Since nearly everyone I worked with had stock options, the "option effect" on corporate campus is cancelled out.

Money is wonderful in that it can make dreams come true. However, in the course of that, having money places you in a defensive position. It's an interesting conundrum. Here you are with a number of zeros padding your confidence, and yet every time you utilize that confidence, you have a huge tax liability.

Just leaving Microsoft cost me 40% of what I thought I had. Hiring the team I wanted to realize my post-Microsoft projects cost me my personal exemptions, the ability to use my mortgage as a tax write-off, and placed me on the hook for more taxes.

In a word, you have to be very careful or you may have to go back to work for someone else. Seriously. My first year's tax liability was more than I had planned to spend in a lifetime. How was I supposed to pay that?

And there are all the other pitfalls. Things don't work out in business ventures. You get phone calls from people who know people you know or did business with, looking for investments in their dreams. You get good at reading poorly written, half-baked proposals and dodging follow-up phone calls.

The best part of having financial resources is your own personal realizations. There's an incredible joy in realizing *your* goals, and nobody or no government agency can take away the joy that your personal fulfillment provides. All the taxes, taxing emotions, flakes, and people without honorable intentions who cross your path do not take away your pride in personal accomplishment.

For me, moving to the U.S. and going to Microsoft was all part of my master plan. I had always wanted to build a kick-ass studio, write an album, work with musicians, engineers, and producers I had always respected, and eventually move into writing music for film. I had also been dabbling in the stock market as a means to finance this money pit known as my music passion.

During my last year at Microsoft I had a pretty demanding schedule. Three jobs took up my day. Up at 6:00 a.m., trading stocks until 10:00 a.m., to Microsoft from 10:00 until 6:00 p.m., then to the studio or rehearsal from 6:00 p.m. until 11:00 p.m., then reading financial periodicals from 11:00 p.m. until 12:00 a.m. Sleep and repeat. Leaving Microsoft gave me more time to devote to both the stock market, which provided me my daily adrenaline fix, and to music, my passion.

I had already completed my first album at the end of 1997 with my band Treason. I featured Alan White and Billy Sherwood of the legendary rock band Yes. Alan is their drummer, holding down that gig for 25 years. I had met Alan in 1993 and we had become great friends—I considered him to be the big brother I never had. We shared love of music, technology, stories of our respective travels, birthdays one day apart, and a love of beer.

Within four months of leaving Microsoft, Yes was scheduled to tour Japan. I had always wanted to experience the Orient and I couldn't have asked for a better tour guide than Yes. I told Alan I was going and next thing you know I was booked in with the band.

Alan and I flew over to Tokyo a couple of days ahead of the crew and we were gonna meet Jon Anderson, Chris Squire and Billy Sherwood the next day. We all met over beers and Billy asked me if I knew why I was there. They had immigration problems with their current keyboard player and asked me if I'd fill in. I thought it was a great gag until they hung the picture of Yes on the wall in the Lexington Queen with my smiling face there in the center.

During this same time I met a wonderful Seattle songwriter named Susan Ennis. Sue was the secret weapon of Ann and Nancy Wilson in Heart. I had written a very moody piece of music called "Spinning" and got a copy of it to Sue. She loved it, and we met to discuss it further. The result was an incredible lyric, melody, and the beginning of my next Treason album. Sue and I wrote the whole album together and featured Ann Wilson on one of the tracks.

I spent about a year and a half writing, recording, and producing the second album, starting a record company, and producing work at several studios. The album turned out the way I have always heard it in my head and I acquired a wealth of legal and business experience during the process, and had the great fortune to work with serious industry heavyweights. This project has truly been a marriage of left and right brain processes, something very rare and fulfilling.

It has been two and a half years since I sat in an office on Microsoft's Corporate Campus. Do I miss it? I find myself scratching my head at my answer, but strangely, I do miss large aspects of it. Two things that come immediately to mind are the constant technology infusion and the large social circle that Microsoft provided. Large corporations have certain advantages that cannot be duplicated in small companies, even your own. And while I love the creative control afforded by my own enterprise, what really keeps me energized on a daily basis is not absolute control, but rather the variety of environments that Microsoft stock has provided me.

It's a nice feeling knowing that I could continue on my own or make a substantial contribution to a corporation, be it Microsoft or another player. Variety is definitely the spice of life, and having the ability to volley between interests, skills, and passions is what makes life worth living.

Anne

Anne's account is a personal one: Microsoft as reflected in her internal world. While she was at Microsoft her smile was sometimes elusive, but now it's dazzling, competing for attention with her deep blue eyes and blonde hair. She's taken her emotional and physical health seriously since leaving Microsoft, completely reshaping her body. She's devoted to her new husband, her freelance writing work, two tiny dogs, exercising, opera, and world travel.

My résumé made the rounds at Microsoft while I was there doing freelance proofreading. Because I spoke French and Spanish, it caught the attention of a manager in the International department. In late 1984, he hired me as an Editorial Assistant in the documentation production group, and I started work early the next year.

On my first day on the job, I watched in consternation as this same manager—now my boss—was carried out the door on a stretcher. He was a high-strung person, and the stress brought on by a screaming fight with another manager resulted in pain that he thought was a heart attack. This was my introduction to the tone of the group.

All that day, I sat alone in my office. I didn't know anyone, and no one knew me or what I was doing there. I had a big stack of paper called the International Documentation Specifications, so I started reading.

It was awful! Sitting there reading that dense mass of printing jargon, I thought there was no way I could do this job; they'd hired me by mistake. I thought about quitting, but that would have been embarrassing, so I came in the next day and kept reading those specs.

I eventually realized the job wasn't so complicated that I couldn't figure it out, and I started talking to people and learning how the place worked. By the time my boss came back a few days later I had some vocabulary down and some questions to ask him. And as I discovered as time went on, this—heart attacks aside—wasn't an uncommon way to begin life at Microsoft: you're thrown into the deep end and it's up to you to swim.

The tone of the department that I'd sensed on my first day was a constant factor. The ongoing and bitter war between the production department (the people who coordinated the work and got the manuals printed) and the localizers (the Europeans and Latin Americans who were responsible for the content) was fueled and fanned by department managers.

In hindsight, it was a classic case of old vs. new, tried-and-true vs. new-and-shiny. The production group had some experienced people who knew how to produce books, but who were not jumping into electronic publishing. The localizers knew nothing about producing manuals but thought that everything should be done the new way.

Even with this underlying tension, individuals forged very good working relationships. In fact, the group became fun. Eventually we got the process worked out and we became early experts at electronic publishing.

It was a small department and we all knew each other. The only Americans in the group were the people in production. We worked with French, Italian, Swedish, German, Dutch, Portuguese, and Spanish-speaking people; language difficulties and clashing cultural assumptions were always part of the mix.

We worked by the seat of our pants and made up procedures when we didn't know how to do something. As long as we got the work done, and as long as the final product looked good, we were free to make whatever decisions we wanted. I loved that.

I found that I was good at working without direction. Change happened constantly and I worked many hours a week. It's all a blur.

I eventually became a Documentation Project Manager. I liked it at first, but like so many at Microsoft who are promoted to management because they are good at the nuts-and-bolts work, I found that managing people—at least managing them well—is a tough, tough job. Today I wouldn't be a manager for a million bucks, but I was different then. I had more faith in my ability to tell other people what to do.

Then International disappeared in a company-wide reorganization and I became a Production Manager in the Office business unit, with managers under me, with production people under them. I became involved in budgets and planning, and was even further removed from the actual work of producing manuals. Then we got reorganized again, and instead of dealing with the silly politics that were going on around me, I quit the company.

✦

Having Microsoft stock started out as unbelievable, a fun joke. Every six months I would get grants of 1000, 1200, 2000 shares. It wasn't worth very much when I got it, but it was neat to get stock. I would daydream about what I'd do when my stock got to be worth a whole lot of money.

Once it started to actually be worth a whole lot of money, it still had an aura of being unreal, a dream, a plaything. Consequently, I didn't take it seriously enough and I talked about it too much with people who didn't need to know. I wish I hadn't.

As time went on and the Microsoft millionaire became a familiar fixture in the local press, I felt sure that my family and my non-Microsoft friends were making assumptions about me. That might not be true, but I was now set apart as "one of them," and I was self-conscious.

It was valuable, though, to talk about the money with my friends at

Microsoft who were in the same boat. We've been able to air feelings about how odd it is suddenly to have the need to earn a living disappear as a central fact of your life. I found that after I left Microsoft, when people asked me what I did, I didn't know what to tell them. My mind would go blank. It was a real shock to me to realize how much I had depended on that work-based identification of myself. Now I was forced to ask myself, if I'm not a manager at Microsoft, what am I?

When you discover one day that you don't have to focus your energy on supporting yourself, it's lovely. But then you have to decide where you *are* going to focus your energy. Daydreams about money don't go far. We all have lots of things we think we would like to do, but in my case the desire to do a lot of them faded when I was actually faced with the opportunity.

It's humbling to realize that if you don't write that novel it's not because you work all the time and don't have time to write, it's because you don't actually want it enough to work at it, or because you've repressed your passion to the extent that you can't reach in and find it anymore. The fabulous garden that I envisioned for myself "when I had time" is still weedy and parched, because it wasn't time that was lacking at all, it was devotion and care. What a discovery!

Money hasn't affected my life the way I expected it to. I thought that having a lot of money would be wonderful because then I wouldn't have to work, but could do fun and creative stuff instead. As it turns out, having a lot of money is wonderful because it allowed me to get to know myself better.

I learned that I actually *like* working. I'm happier working, and I work full-time as a freelance writer. Every day includes a challenge, so every day I get confirmation that I can take care of myself in this world; I don't have to feel at the mercy of the stock market. Working helps me feel well rounded, self-sufficient, and competent.

I learned that in focusing all my time and energy on my work life, I'd let my spirit all but atrophy, and that being a whole, centered, and authentic person takes time, thought, and work.

I learned that I'd assumed an identity based almost entirely on my life at Microsoft, and that that identity was incomplete, at best. I remember sitting in a restaurant shortly after I left Microsoft and vowing to my friend that I was never again going to laugh at a joke that I didn't think was funny; that I was never going to profess an opinion that I didn't actually have; and that from now on if I didn't know the answer to a question I was going to say, "I don't know!"

Those things seem so basic now, but to me at the time they were declarations of independence and the first step towards dismantling the Microsoft soldier and rebuilding my genuine self. I had a lot of work to do.

The whole experience of working at Microsoft was life changing. While I was there, I became a lot more aware of myself and my talents and limitations and my ambition or lack of ambition, what things make me happy, and what kind of feedback and appreciation I need to be happy. When I left, the money I came away with gave me even more opportunity to grow and to know myself.

I'm glad that I ended up at Microsoft. My dearest friends today are people I met there. My life is the way it is because of Microsoft. I never had any ambition to work in the software industry. I never had any ambition to be rich. I just landed in a place that allowed me to work hard and then rewarded me for that work.

Scott

Scott's face is one you see in paintings from the Middle Ages, oval and smooth with slightly hooded eyes, medium build, medium height, medium hair color, medium eye color. He's a quiet guy, friendly, low-key, and a good communicator. He talks about his career in technical writing, questions Microsoft's corporate attitude, and contemplates the changes money made in his life, from nosy questions from neighbors to helping others with their personal finance issues.

I landed my job at Microsoft during a camping trip in 1985. My sister and brother-in-law invited me on their annual summer solstice camping trip, a Bacchanalian bash in the woods. My sister introduced me to her friend Debbie, who managed a group of technical writers at Microsoft. We talked only briefly that weekend, but I made sure to get her business card.

I soon called and asked her if she had any job openings. Debbie asked me why I wanted to work as a technical writer.

"I want to write more," I told her, "and I want to manage my own time." Debbie later confessed that my statement about time management hooked her. She took me to lunch, looked over my writing samples, and offered me a paid internship.

I was soon working as a technical writing intern for Microsoft's Operating Systems division. Our group wrote instruction manuals to accompany the operating systems Microsoft sold to computer manufacturers, who in turn rewrote the documentation to fit their specific products. I was the tenth employee in the department, the third male, and one of approximately 800 company workers.

I didn't feel like the typical employee. Many of them seemed to be Ivy League graduates who actually knew something about computers. Most of them seemed to have aimed for employment at Microsoft for a long time. I was surrounded by intelligent, educated, motivated, and energetic people on a daily basis. In comparison, my entire computing experience came in one summer's use of Whitman College's writing lab featuring a single Kaypro computer running the CPM operating system and WordStar word-processing program. I felt like a remedial freshman allowed to play in the senior physics laboratory.

Debbie showed me to an interior office, long and narrow, with a solid oak desk at the far end. On top of the desk were a terminal and nine volumes of documentation. That first day I read so much polysyllabic gunk about scripts and shells and line editors that I got on the afternoon bus heading in the wrong direction.

I knew it was the wrong direction. I didn't care. I needed the ride out to the edge of the county and back to recover.

Eventually, the work challenged but did not overwhelm me. I learned that there are productive weeks and down days. I discovered that less than a quarter of my time went to writing words that customers would actually read and use. Planning, analyzing, drafting, testing, revising, and reviewing all contributed to the finished product. Learning the scope and flow of writing work at Microsoft helped me feel more comfortable when I eventually decided to write on my own.

In the 1980's Microsoft earned a reputation for long work hours. That's accurate but not complete. Everyone there worked long hours at some point, but not all the time. A lot of the long days didn't contain more than eight or nine hours of work.

Many younger employees stayed at work all day because all their friends were there. Many of them came from outside of Washington. They had little or no family or outside friends when they moved to Redmond. Many were living in apartments on their own, often for the first time. Outside of work, they had few connections to people and community. At work, though, they were surrounded by people of similar age, education, race, class, employment, and taste.

It was not uncommon for these folks to spend an hour or two in the middle of the day drinking espresso in a cafeteria, playing sandlot volleyball, or even enjoying a long bike ride around the foothills of the Cascades. Sure, they were at work for more than twelve hours that day, but at least two hours were spent completely away from their desks.

Microsoft encouraged this lifestyle. They recruited straight out of college. They refer to the corporate headquarters as "campus." The building interiors looked like college dormitories—long hallways with many doors, punctuated by kitchenettes and small lounges. Campus included treed paths, ponds, cafeterias, playing fields, exercise equipment, and locker rooms.

Towards the end of my employment, I grew critical of the company's self-absorption. One example of corporate narcissism came when everyone who worked in product development was invited out to the soccer fields at the center of the corporate campus. There we enjoyed free barbecue, soda, music, and entertainment, and a carnival atmosphere usually reserved for the annual Christmas party.

Once the crowd was sufficiently warmed up, the Vice President of Human Resources took the stage. He personally expressed his thanks for our hard work and dedication. He'd devised a new way for Microsoft to recognize our efforts. I expected a new policy for sabbatical leave. Maybe we'd get extra vacation days upon completing a project. There'd been plenty of employee requests for such benefits to help us recover after working weeks of unpaid overtime to complete a project.

The VP held up a slab of Lucite. "This," he said like Moses displaying the tablets, "is the Ship-It Award."

Each one of us would receive one engraved with our name and a statement of thanks from the company. In the future, whenever we finished a new product, we would receive a small tag with the name of the product that we could affix to our plastic slab. Over the years, seeing all the tags would remind us of how much Microsoft appreciated our contributions.

I was baffled and insulted. He honestly thought that a plaque would make me feel better about the stressful weeks and years? All the award would do was remind me of how much of my existence I gave to Microsoft. How many hours of meetings and pages of design proposals were wasted on this idea?

Back in my office, I emailed the person in charge of the new Ship-It bureaucracy, asking how I could opt out. Evidently I was not alone. Within a couple days email arrived from the VP's assistant. Through a typographical error, the title of the email referred to the Shit-It Award. It detailed how the award program would work and included the option of not participating. I returned my lump of Lucite per the instructions.

My colleague Mike took his award home and burned it in his fireplace. According to him, Lucite burns with surprising speed and heat. If he hadn't had glass doors on his fireplace, his entire condominium building might have burned down.

As a manager, at the end of my Microsoft career I got to determine raises and bonuses during the employee evaluation process. Not only were employees scored individually, I found out, but also ordered from most to least valuable across the entire department. I found it hard to say that this person was more valuable or important that one. Once employees were ranked individually and collectively, we assigned percentage raises and bonuses according to corporate guidelines. Our distribution of percentages was supposed to resemble a bell curve and not deviate from a mandated average percent. Outside of manager's meetings we were supposed to encourage team behavior among these people. The review process negated that idea.

Because of time constraints the managers at times determined ratings, raises, and bonuses before any employees submitted their review forms. This seemed shady at best. In particular, I felt one of my editors got screwed out of the raise and bonus she deserved. The review system was partly to blame, but so was my timidity and inexperience at management. I still feel badly about that.

As a Microsoft employee, my best way to save money for future writing was stock options—the chance to buy shares of the company's common stock tomorrow at today's price. With time and work and luck, the value of the stock would rise while the option price would remain fixed. Any increase in value translated into money in my pocket.

As part of my November 1986 employee review the company awarded me the option to buy 1000 shares of Microsoft stock at $30 a share. The option took full effect, or vested, gradually over the next four and a half years and remained good for ten years. At a few subsequent employee reviews I was granted additional options, though never as large as the first.

The company posted the stock price on the computer network every weekday afternoon, usually around 3 p.m. Its appearance was something of a watershed. If the afternoon was going well—no deadlines hanging over my head, no meetings, little or no email to answer—the posting of the closing stock price meant soon I'd be commuting homeward, into the sunset, across one of Seattle's floating bridges spanning Lake Washington. It's hard to imagine a more scenic traffic jam.

But, if work was going awfully—another twelve-hour day spent rewriting chapters to accommodate last minute redesigning of the software—I would close my office door and repeatedly check for the arrival of the day's quote. Once the stock market delivered a figure, I'd enter it into a spreadsheet and let the magic of computers do the math in a nanosecond: subtract option price from current price, multiply the remainder by number of shares, deduct percentages for income taxes and retirement savings, and display the final result at the bottom of the page.

For a few minutes I'd fantasize about how I could live on that much money if I quit right then. But at that point the thought of quitting was just a crutch to get me through the day. I'd sigh, close the spreadsheet, and return to work.

On rare and wonderful afternoons, maybe once every two years, email would arrive announcing a stock split. People would whoop out of their offices, jump down the halls high-fiving each other, and tell those still at their desks to check their mail. A split meant that the board of directors had decided to give everyone who held stock in the company, say, another share for every share they already owned. This doubled the number of shares, but made each one worth half as much. On the face of it, no change in value and no big deal.

But a split affects stock options as well as stock. That 1000 shares I was granted at $30 would become 2000 shares at $15. As the stock kept splitting, my grant would become 3000 shares at $10, then 6000 shares at $5, and so on. If the stock reaches $100 a share, splits down to $50, and then rises again to $100, the value of the stock options has doubled. Multiply that by thousands of shares, and you get some serious money.

When the announcement of a split arrived, it was hard to keep in mind that not everyone around me had stock options. Of course, all the programmers and managers did but newer writers, editors, and testers didn't. Neither did the administrative assistants, invariably young women doing the yeoman's work of keeping everything in the organization running.

Over the years the stock-option divide became more apparent and I tried to tone down any discussion or celebration regarding stock. People still celebrated, though, whenever a split was announced. My colleague Christopher referred to the whole spectacle as the "financial freak show": paper millionaires with egos like large paper lanterns.

I know plenty of people inside Microsoft and out who worked as hard as I did or harder and did not receive what I received. The thought of "earning" the amount of money I did for the work I performed seems absurd.

At the start of my sixth year working for Microsoft, my wife Shannon and I finally moved into a house we had been remodeling. We were out in our front yard when Stacy, the very Republican real-estate agent who lived next door, introduced herself. She asked what we did for a living. Upon hearing that we worked for Microsoft, she excused herself and went back inside her house. She returned with a catalog of luxury homes that she thought were suitable for Microsoft employees and wanted to know if we knew of anyone looking for a house. She eventually got around to asking Shannon, "Are you guys Microsoft millionaires? I was just wondering."

Shannon paused for a moment while I marveled at the audacity of the question. Maybe that's what it takes to succeed in real estate. Shannon sat back on her heels and said, "If I were a millionaire, would I be out here on my hands and knees in the dirt pulling weeds?" This rhetorical defense silenced Stacy, but the truth was that Shannon would have been out there even if she did have a million dollars.

Another lesson that Shannon and I learned concerned image. One workday we stopped by an appliance store near the Microsoft campus. I don't remember what we wanted to buy. I do remember finding the item and deciding that the price was a little above what we'd planned on paying. It wasn't so high, though, that some bonus thrown into the deal, like a free extended warranty, wouldn't even things out. We took our item to the sales desk, said we'd like to purchase it, and asked if we could get an extended warranty as part of the listed price.

The sales clerk looked down at my coat, which had *Microsoft* embroidered on it. The company had given me the coat for participating in shipping Excel version 4. He then looked me in the eye and said no.

Shannon and I knew we had no bargaining power. We bought the item anyway. Even now, years later, I check my clothes for logos before making a major purchase.

For quite a while I planned on quitting in August 1994. By that time the current corporate reorganization would be complete, the next software projects under way, the departmental budget complete, another round of employee evaluations done, and my stock options dwindling. It would also be nine years, nearly to the day, of my starting as an intern. I just couldn't see holding out for ten years to receive a briefcase I'd never use and another week's vacation. One night at the beginning of March 1994, though, something caught me on my way to bed. Spring fever, intuition, full moon—I don't know. This something whispered to me with the question "What if you left before August?"

That night I dreamt of flying. I jog through the myriad gray corridors of Microsoft. I run out the side door of a building and into the parking lot. I sprint towards the side of a pickup truck and with a steeplechase leap I place one foot on the edge of the truck bed, push off and rise into the air, soaring over the campus, swooping down on people walking in the sunshine between buildings, sliding over forests of Douglas fir, over stretches of white-capped oceans, over countryside and cities I'd never seen before. In the morning I woke euphoric.

My last day at Microsoft was Wednesday, March 23rd, 1994. I fit in final company-paid trips to the doctor, dentist, and optometrist and came away with reading glasses and new fillings.

My boss sent email, titled with just my name, announcing my departure and inviting people to the requisite going-away party. Our administrative assistant ordered a sheet cake and reserved a conference room. People arrived at the appointed time, took a piece of cake, and stood around the perimeter of the room. No one ever sat down at going-away parties. My colleagues roasted me with anecdotes from nine years of employment. When the party was over, I carried my last box of personal belongings from my office to my car and commuted home.

✦

I returned to Microsoft as a freelance writer, a corporate immigrant. The orange background of my new Microsoft ID badge had the word

"Contractor" printed on it. The badge was my work visa. I could legally earn money here, but the benefits of citizenship did not apply to me. No more raise and bonus twice a year. The generosity of my former medical and retirement plans was gone, along with membership in the nearby health club. Participation in Microsoft social clubs or athletic leagues was prohibited. I couldn't walk into the company store and purchase software at a 90% discount.

On the other hand, none of the strictures applied to me either. I could ignore nearly all memos, forms, and meetings. I could comfortably despise my supervisor or my work because I didn't have a personal stake in its success. If someone wanted me to work overtime, they'd have to pay time and a half for it. I could leave this place at the end of the contract—no more staring at an eternal horizon of project after project. And I was free to question, at least to myself, everything around me.

Computers and their programs are merely tools and thus are morally neutral. I knew the networking, word processing, and number-crunching products I helped produce enabled many noble tasks. Nonprofit agencies use Microsoft products to help deliver goods and services to people in need. Hospitals and universities use Microsoft products to help people live richer lives. Yet I also suspected that Colombian cocaine cartels use Microsoft spreadsheets to calculate their profits.

I'm very thankful for my post-Microsoft life. The skills I learned, the confidence I gained, the friends I made, and yes, the money I received, still form a large part of my life. Mostly I consider my life a success thus far. I have people in my life that I love, work that I enjoy, and contentment with myself and my surroundings. I had those at Microsoft, as well.

Success hasn't been about money for me. I still think about money, plan about it, organize and wonder about it. Success hasn't been about achievement, either. Yes, I've traveled, started studying Italian, and had my creative writing published, but by themselves these mean little.

Success for me lies in continually trying to be the type of person who's thoughtful, kind, curious, humorous, expressive. That type of success anyone can achieve, anywhere. It's the type of success that will keep our sanity as a society. It's also the type of success that I found in many of the people at Microsoft.

Working at Microsoft was definitely worth it. Even though I attended a well-respected liberal arts college, I feel that Microsoft taught me more about how to approach and solve problems. Being surrounded by intelligent people and demanding, engaging work raised my intelligence. Some of those people became very close friends.

All the goal setting and project planning at Microsoft gave me confidence in myself and in setting goals. Since leaving Microsoft, I've set goals for myself: finishing graduate school in writing; completing and marketing a novel; writing publishable work in fiction, nonfiction, and poetry. I set financial goals, as well, to guide my management of the money I received: goals for spending, saving, researching investments, and donating to charitable causes.

But working that hard and succeeding also taught me that there's more to life than work. I'm a person first. Nurturing spirit and character and kindness is more challenging and rewarding than any project.

TC

He can be reserved on first meeting, but his blue eyes shine as he listens carefully without interrupting. TC is naturally muscular despite long hours at the keyboard and a complete disinterest in sports. He scrambled to put himself through college, the first one in his family to do so. Reflecting his eclectic range of interests, he spent the first year studying architecture, then switched to physics. TC had a rags-to-riches experience: at the startup he was part of, "will work for food" was the deal until Microsoft came calling.

The way I came to the company is about as far as from "graduated from college and got hired by Microsoft" as you can get. I was part of a small startup in California named Dynamical Systems Research that Microsoft acquired in 1986.

But that's the short answer.

I've taken only one computer science course in my life. It was a Fortran class I was required to take as part of my major in physics. I vividly remember walking out of the computer center late one evening very frustrated, and I shouted into the night, "I will never, never, never program computers for a living."

So I ended up getting my bachelor's degree in physics with the idea that I would somehow use it to become an inventor. A pretty vague plan, I must admit. I got an internship with Hughes Research Laboratories in Malibu, where I was a nobody with a lowly bachelor's degree working in one of the top ivory-tower research labs in the country. It was clear that over time almost any kind of pure or applied research would be possible if I proved myself worthy. It was literally a dream come true. I had stumbled into a situation where I could become an inventor and be paid well for it.

Although the work I did wasn't classified, I was uncomfortable working for a major component of the military-industrial complex. This was a big dilemma for me, because at Hughes I was like a kid in a candy store.

Eventually, after that first summer plus one year, my unease won out and I decided to escape to graduate school. I left Hughes with the promise of a job every summer break if I wanted it.

As the end of my first year of graduate school approached I wasn't happy. The root of my interest in physics seemed to be getting lost in the details. I was not happy contemplating how long it was going to be before I would get to work on interesting things of my own choosing.

About that time a fellow teaching assistant told me about Dynamical Systems Research, a small software company in Oakland being started by a bunch of physicists from Princeton. He had been told wondrous tales of how successful they might be. This startup was paying only in stock, but despite needing paychecks, we both decided to teach ourselves 8086 assembler language at night and try to get hired there for the summer on the chance the company might take off. It seemed like an adventure.

Now we had to learn 8086 assembler and produce something with it that would get us hired at DSR. We only had a few weeks and still had our classes and teaching assistant duties to attend to as well. Thus began a too-long trend in serious burning of the midnight oil. I had clearly forgotten the promise I'd screamed into the night a few years before.

Over the course of about a month I managed to write a simple but functional spreadsheet in 8086 assembly language from scratch. My friend wrote a Basic interpreter. We sent them off to we-knew-not-who at this startup. A week or so later, they said we should come up for an interview. At our own expense, of course. So we did.

They "hired" us. Our pay would be an undisclosed amount of stock in the company for work accomplished. We could live in their "headquarters." This was a condemned house on a hill in Oakland. It had holes in the walls and the floors were unfinished. There was very little sheetrock anywhere, nothing but decayed lathe and plaster.

No one was supposed to be living in this firetrap, but for over a year we worked and lived out of this place that was more suited to being a haunted house than a place of business or a residence. Is it necessary to say that we were very naïve?

There were two bedrooms with three or four mattresses in each one. The house was freezing cold in the winter. It had no heating but it did have electricity to run the computers. We ate spare communal meals cooked by our CEO's wife—if you were late to dinner, you went hungry. It was definitely some kind of adventure, although not quite the kind we had fantasized about.

The plan for the company was this. IBM had developed a character-based windowing interface for its PCs called Topview. But what about all the clone makers like DEC and HP that wanted a piece of the personal computer pie? How would they compete with IBM's Topview? They would buy our clone of Topview, of course. Our clone would be smaller and faster than Topview and would provide the same functionality.

We would laugh all the way to the bank. Maybe we'd fix the holes in the walls and have some heating put in. Heck, maybe we'd even get our own places to live.

Eventually we managed to move into a better house near Piedmont. Not that we were making any money, since none of the clone makers had actually bought anything from us yet, but we had investors and they put up enough additional money to get a place that had real walls.

Despite the new and improved digs, things were getting dicey. It had been over a year and I was living off a small and quickly diminishing savings account. The free food ended when we moved to the new house and the company started paying us stipends to buy our own food. This was the princely sum of $28 a week.

Realistically, however, this couldn't go on. I was broke. I was tired of the lifestyle. I was even getting tired of some of the people—we were just together too much. I decided to leave and told our CEO, Nathan Myhrvold, I was leaving in one month. He didn't like it, probably because this was exactly what he worried about most: a slave revolt, but what was he going to do, offer me a big fat raise? And then Microsoft called.

It was Steve Ballmer on the phone. He'd like to come talk to us, would that be okay? Well, yeah, sure. So we took down our dartboard—*Time Magazine* with Bill Gates on the cover—and Steve flew down from Redmond.

He took Nathan out to dinner while the rest of us stayed home and ate bread and drank water and wondered what was going down. When they came back our chief had a question for the tribe. How did we feel about moving to Seattle and getting paid real salaries?

As it turns out, Microsoft was in negotiations with IBM over Windows 1.0. IBM didn't want to license Windows unless it had something they called a Topview emulator in it. Microsoft knew next to nothing about Topview and the whole idea sounded crazy since Windows is a graphical, not character-based, interface, but in those days it was giant IBM and little ol' Microsoft. If IBM wanted a Topview emulator, a Topview emulator Microsoft would promise. But how to deliver? It so happened that someone at Microsoft had read an *InfoWeek* article about our work and brought it to the attention of Steve.

They flew us all up to Redmond to wine and dine us. Oh, and interview us. The interviews really weren't anything of the sort, especially of the sort that Microsoft became known for. We could obviously code, we were eight warm bodies, and we had that Topview clone in our pockets. My interviews were more like friendly chats with three or four people who told me what a great place to work Microsoft was and what a great place to live Seattle was. I personally needed little convincing: I was broke and needed a real job real soon.

They kept us together at first and gave us one wing of Building Four on the brand-new Redmond campus. There were only four small cross-shaped buildings then, set in the middle of a forest. Sadly, today the forest is pretty much gone. And now that original cluster of four buildings is like a punctuation mark in a paragraph. Recently I heard the sad news that these buildings are now scheduled for demolition.

We were still working long hours but not quite so long as at DSR. But the very real anxiety that goes with knowing that you are rapidly descending into abject poverty had suddenly vanished. That first paycheck seemed magical. Okay, I thought, so maybe I *am* going to program computers for a living. Maybe it won't be such a bad thing after all.

At first being at Microsoft seemed like a worker's paradise. The stock was in a publicly traded company and we knew how much we were getting and when we would get it. Imagine that. And having a place I called home that was separate from both workplace and co-workers was blissful.

Although the hours were long, there was so much more flexibility and privacy of every kind, such as everyone having their own office, that my first year or so at Microsoft seemed to unfold at an almost relaxed pace even if from the outside it looked crazy. I would often come in as "late" as 9:30 a.m. but not leave until 8 or 9 p.m., and there were plenty of longer days. I remember several times being on campus, mostly in my office programming or debugging, for more than 24 hours at a stretch.

When we arrived from DSR, most of us didn't even know the C programming language. We were 8086 assembly programmers. But learning computer languages isn't terribly hard. It's much easier than becoming fluent in a foreign language, for example. So we all quickly broadened our scope and learned C (there's a pun for the programmers).

✦

Other than a few difficult bosses, the people were great, meaning nice, helpful, competent and hard working, the latter to a fault. Despite the very young average age (I was a bit old at 28 when I started), most people quickly got caught up in the "work 'til you drop" mentality that was, naturally, actively encouraged by management.

Ironically, the one close friend I gained in my time at Microsoft had a bit of a problem with the *work, work, work* mentality. If I didn't need to ask someone a question I pretty much stayed in my office coding or debugging. It's just my style. But this guy really liked to socialize. He would make a couple of rounds per day to several friends, dropping in just to chat.

Of course, management was not unaware of his social tendencies. They thought he should be working more (though by any normal standard he worked plenty) and so should the people he was "interrupting." But from my perspective his brief visits were a high point of the day. I am sure I would have burnt out even sooner without them. He's the one person I actively stayed in touch with after I left and we remain good friends.

Another person I really enjoyed working with was my immediate boss for my last few years. Pete was more than a little irreverent about most things and since this matched my own personality I felt comfortable reporting to him. He also had a dry and wicked sense of humor, which helped with the long hours and the pressure to accomplish lots in record time.

The other really great thing about Pete was that he took me under his wing. He had been there long enough, knew enough people, and had enough experience that he could move to any group that interested him. After a year or two, or sometimes just six months, he would get bored with whatever we were working on and he'd go hunting for a new technical lead position. This happened a couple of times after I started reporting to him. I would be disappointed at first because it meant I would suddenly have a new boss and they were never as good as Pete. Too serious, too full of themselves, or whatever.

Then Pete would show up a few weeks after going off to his new group, close the door to my office, and suggest that I join his new group. Of course he didn't have to push hard at all. It wasn't just that it was flattering to be asked to follow him to his new group; I was typically getting seriously bored and considering quitting before I'd really vested enough stock when Pete would show up like this. Being able to follow him as he moved around the company definitely extended the number of years I stayed.

✦

Regardless of the project I was working on, my time at Microsoft was spent almost exclusively with other programmers and testers, i.e. technical people. They were always smart, usually hard working, often more loyal than I felt, and occasionally arrogant. But the arrogance was concentrated in a few individuals, unlike the talent.

Everyone seemed aware that we were part of something unusual. I don't mean that we were at Microsoft. I mean that we were very much aware of working at the edge of the brand new technology of the microprocessor and that it was and still is world-changing stuff.

That's an exciting thought to have in the back of your mind as you're writing code or tracking down bugs. I think this is central to what drives people in the high technology industry, both then and now.

Nevertheless, I have to admit to feeling dissatisfied at Microsoft almost from the beginning, once the novelty of having a real salary and a separate place to live wore off. The truth is that I didn't really find my work interesting. I always wanted to be working at a higher level but felt that I didn't have the experience or clout to get out of the small-picture programming trench I felt like I was in. As the joy of having a real job faded I became increasingly bored being in that trench.

I like work that combines a big-picture vision with detailed implementation work. But I wasn't in the big-picture club at Microsoft. And even if I had been, it would have necessarily been a business-oriented big picture. My personal bent is more academic. I want to be working on a research edge more than a business edge. A business view of innovation is ultimately about getting and keeping market share. A research view of innovation is more about pushing the pure possibilities of what can be done with the technology. In a company these two views are related but they are not the same thing.

I was also suffering from a kind of impatience with the pace and direction of the PC revolution swirling about us. Here we were with the amazingly flexible technology of the microprocessor, *the most flexible general-purpose technology ever invented*, and all we were doing was writing operating systems, compilers, spreadsheets, and word processors. Of course this was just the beginning of the PC revolution and these kinds of things were the logical first steps.

These application categories were truly revolutionary from a business and consumer point of view and highly lucrative as a result. But every time I used some application I quickly found myself wanting to do things with it that it just couldn't do. Applications then and now are mostly monolithic in the sense that they do some particular set of things they are hard coded to do. That set may seem large and rich but it is also essentially fixed in stone. The next version may do more but what *more* means and when it is available is decided by the company that creates it, whether that's Microsoft or IBM or Adobe. And the new feature set is just as fixed in stone as the previous one. Standard software comes not just with features but with an even bigger set of limitations.

What I wanted to work on was a different kind of application. I wanted applications that would be more like a collaboration with the user, designed to allow the user or a user community to add features and in some sense co-create the application. At the time I didn't really know how this might be achieved but just thinking about this kind of thing excited me more than my actual work did.

My problem was that Microsoft certainly wasn't working on anything like this, not only because such a paradigm might not be as lucrative as one in which the software company totally controls the feature set and user experience, but also because the software industry as a whole had not yet reached such a stage.

Over a decade later, certain parts of the industry are beginning to move in this direction with the emergence of languages like Java and collaborative open source projects like Linux. I just didn't see a way to pursue this out-of-the-box interest at Microsoft. It called for a research oriented position, not the coding and debugging jobs I was being assigned. Eventually a real research division was started, headed by my former boss Nathan, no less. But by the time this happened I had been bored and frustrated for almost four years, and in my heart I was already on the way out.

So why did I let myself be bored and frustrated for four years? Why did I feel so stuck? If I'd understood this better would I have been able to do something about it and stay longer at Microsoft? In retrospect I think part of the issue was that I was still, completely unconsciously, acting like a graduate student among the professors instead of acting like a full employee of Microsoft. The DSR company structure had been left intact and I accepted that too easily when in fact I didn't like being in that structure.

I think I didn't adjust fast enough to the possibilities around me partly because I didn't feel properly prepared. Everything I knew was self taught and there were plenty of things I knew little about. I felt like I didn't really fit in to the larger world of all the other programmers at Microsoft. I felt like it would be a joke to go knock on the Excel group's door, for example. I'd never felt like this at Hughes Research Labs because regardless of what I didn't know, my academic path was the appropriate one.

Even more important though was the fact that I never thought of being at Microsoft as following my true path. I always felt like I was on a detour from the realms of my real interests in science, inventions, and art. I had always struggled with finding a way to combine my interests in science and art. Starting out in college as an architecture major and switching to physics was one expression of that struggle. I didn't see being at Microsoft as furthering my search for that synthesis. Instead, I increasingly came to see it as doing time while I vested enough stock to allow me to pursue that synthesis on my own, later, somewhere else.

✦

When I called in rich, I called in early and wasn't really very rich but thoughts of more money couldn't soothe my boredom anymore. It would have been different to be expected to work all those hours if I was working on something—anything—that actually interested me. So I walked away from quite a lot of unvested stock (just under a million dollars net in 1992) after a relatively short six years.

Money can't buy satisfaction unless your highest value is money. I value being fully engaged and interested in what I'm spending the hours of my life doing. I increasingly felt I was sacrificing this for money. There seemed to be no place for me to discover, let alone follow, my software muse, let alone my science or my art muse at Microsoft. I had to leave.

Once I left, I was in heaven! Now I was free to do pretty much whatever I wanted to do. I had the choice to not work for a while and possibly, if I was careful, forever.

The first thing I did was to call family and friends and tell them I'd finally done it. My father's reaction was typical.

"You did *what*? You really quit your job? What are you going to do? Where are you going to work?"

His reaction was understandable. This kind of thing simply didn't happen in my parents' or any previous generation. My parents both worked hard. My mother went back to college to get a better job as a nurse and my dad worked two jobs for many years, one in the office at Western Pacific Railroad and a second in the office at a local cannery. They provided well for all four of us children, but money was always an issue and a source of tension.

The children of the not-rich do not normally rocket out of their parents' caste before middle age. This was a new phenomenon born of the profit margins of high technology and of stock options no longer being a benefit reserved for top executives.

One small but tricky problem of quitting work at such a young age is the dilemma of what to tell people. Is there any more common question for a new acquaintance to ask than what you do? Saying I was retired didn't work for me. In the first place, it didn't feel right. I intended to work again someday but hopefully for myself. And it sounds so odd when there's no gray hair or wrinkles showing. I settled for saying I was self-employed and if any further inquiries were made I said I was a programmer. It covered the bases of past and possible future even though it didn't strictly apply to the present.

I was ready to enjoy my newfound freedom. At first I didn't really want to do much but sleep in and read and ride my bike. I was pretty burnt out. I needed to be as ambition-free as possible for a while. A few months after quitting I started playing around with painting. I'd always been interested in drawing and painting but had no time to pursue this while I was working. Now I started buying canvases and paints and just playing around. This didn't lead to any actual art, but it did lead to buying a new house.

One day on my way to buy art supplies I saw a sign that said "Open House: Lake View" so I decided to take a look. The house turned out to be really unusual and did in fact have a beautiful view of Lake Washington from high up on a hill. The house had odd angles and tall, light-filled spaces and a huge artist's studio.

When I was a kid, I wanted to be an architect. I spent a lot of time designing homes way beyond the means of my parents. I'd started college as an architecture major at the University of Oregon. A chill went up my neck when I walked in this house because it was a lot like one of my favorite childhood designs. I wanted it immediately, and for the first time in my life I could indulge such a desire. I felt a little guilty since I certainly didn't need such a large house but within a week I'd made an offer that was accepted a few days later.

So I spent the next few months moving. This was definitely odd.

Just six years before I had less than five hundred dollars to my name. And now I was paying cash for a new house a few months after quitting my job. It felt surreal. It still feels surreal.

A few years after quitting I was no longer feeling burnt out and I was beginning to want to do something serious again. I toyed with the idea of going back to graduate school but realized I didn't want that kind of pressure or schedule again so soon. And I wanted to feel like I was contributing something to society at large by working on something that actually grabbed me.

A danger of financial freedom coming early in life is that you don't *have* to do anything. There is no external structure for what you do with your day. There aren't even the usual consequences if you decide to do nothing at all. I know of people who've stayed at Microsoft from fear of how they would fill their days if they left.

In 1994 or so, I went to a scientific conference at Arizona State University in Tucson. There I met someone with a background in film and video production. I had been thinking about working in documentaries for about a year, and had even thought about going to film school. A great deal of interesting stuff is going on all the time that is mostly ignored by the major media. I wanted to look into ways to bring some of the most interesting material to a wider audience. It also seemed to me that with the explosion of television channels, anybody with high production value and interesting content could find a market.

We started a small business to produce documentaries on various unusual subjects. After getting set up, we decided that our first project would be about some unusual research concerning connections between Jewish mysticism and the origin of the Hebrew alphabet being conducted by a non-profit organization called The Meru Foundation.

Although I am not conventionally religious, I do find the origins and beliefs of all spiritual traditions fascinating. Meru's work was very interesting but quite complex, and begged for a documentary with great visuals and animations to explain it to a non-technical audience.

I had always been interested in computer graphics and animation, so the project seemed like a good fit for me. I had already been spending a fair amount of time playing around with various graphics packages for my own artistic reasons and this was a good reason to learn more.

We went around the country interviewing various people who knew of Meru's work, ranging from academics at major universities to rabbis with knowledge of Kabbala, the Jewish mystical tradition. This was great fun and very interesting but gradually I came to realize that my business partner and I were not a good match. Despite believing the project was a worthy one, I eventually decided I could no longer work with my partner and I stopped working on the project. Nevertheless, during this time I met a lot of incredibly interesting people and made some very close friends.

It's funny how you start off down one path and when you reach the end, what you got out of the journey may be very, very different from what you expected at the start. These "surprise endings" are one of life's greatest pleasures for me.

In retrospect the fruitless documentary-making stint did serve a purpose. In a way it brought me full circle. I was more interested than ever in computer graphics applications. But once again, the more I used various applications the more frustrated I became with their limitations and lack of real extensibility. And I was getting tired of having to use so many different programs to do what I wanted to do. At heart I'm an engineer/inventor. I am always looking at things from the perspective of how they might be improved. So I started thinking about creating the program I wanted instead of complaining that no such program existed. I decided to turn my frustration into action.

What I wanted was an object oriented graphics program that in a sense did nothing graphical. It would just be a scaffolding or framework that could read and write various image file formats and that relied on extensions to do the actual drawing of graphical elements, whether that was drawing a circle or rendering a 3-D scene. But the scaffolding would also be able to "inspect" these extensions and thereby allow complex interactions between extensions without the extensions themselves needing to know anything about each other. The extensions would be relatively simple, but the scaffolding would create a context for powerful synergy between them. My idea was to create the scaffolding and a basic set of extensions, and encourage a community of interested users to write ever more sophisticated extensions.

Then the whole software world changed. Java appeared and soon after that Linux came on the scene. Though I don't agree with a lot of the "software should be free" zealotry that came along with these developments, the kind of "communityware" I'd been dreaming of was actually starting to come into being in some fashion.

So these days I spend a lot of my free time writing this program. I've been working on it for about four years now and I hope to release it in another year or so. Regardless of what comes of this work I'll finally have the program I wanted but couldn't buy. And if other people with similar interests see value in this approach, maybe it will serve as a small contribution to a geeky little niche of society at large. If it turns out that way, that will be much more satisfying than calling in rich ever was.

Mary

Mary is a loyal boss and friend. She's slim and strong and wears almost nothing but Levis and T-shirts. She had the will and the drive to leave the farm, but her connection to family took her back once she made her fortune. She was a stealth worker, quietly establishing a great reputation as her management responsibilities and her skills grew. A telling moment: she wanted so badly to move to corporate headquarters that she took the risk of quitting her job at a Microsoft subsidiary, determined to find a place for herself in Redmond.

I put myself through college by working on a family farm in Middle of Nowhere, South Dakota. My aunt reminded me daily that I might as well get used to getting up at 5 or 6 a.m., noting that at least I didn't have to put on those dreaded nylons and a skirt like I would when I got a real job. She was so wrong.

It was 1989. I was working in a fourth-rate computer clone company in Dallas that was going no place, so I started looking for another job. I answered so many ads that it was hard to keep them all straight. I got home one night to a message from a guy named Paul at the local Microsoft sales office. "Microsoft, hum, that's the company that makes DOS, right?" That was about all I knew about it. But then again, back then, there wasn't much more to tell.

I'll never forget the interview. I kept thinking that I wanted to work in a place like this, with a view and impressive offices, not to mention free pop. Paul asked me if I knew Mac Word. I lied—nobody used Mac Word back then, WordPerfect dominated the market. I said I'd used the PC version but it'd been some time ago. Then he put me to the test on a Mac. I panicked at first, but sure enough, it was close and I figured it out. I got the job.

I'd been in Dallas two years at that point, long enough to know it wasn't the city for me. And I'd been at MS for a year and knew that was exactly where I wanted to be, only not in Dallas.

I decided to move to corporate headquarters and thought Seattle would be a good thing after Dallas. I decided this having never set foot in Washington—it was a leap of faith. The only problem was I was an Administrative Assistant, which was not the type of job that MS would fly you around to interview for. So I flew out to Redmond at my own expense to interview...and didn't get the job.

Still, I figured if I could just get out there, I could land a position. I handed in my resignation and kept looking. Before my final day, I got a phone interview that would change my life forever. I remember sitting with my feet up on my desk, feeling confident and at ease with the person on the other end of the phone. She hired me from that interview and off to Redmond I went to be a Group Assistant in the International Product Group.

My new manager in Redmond was the best teacher one could ever have. She knew how the system worked and how to work around it. She taught me to speak my mind and not be afraid of what that meant, a trait that stuck with me throughout my career, much to many people's dismay, I'm certain. She smoked like a chimney, swore like a truck driver, and dressed like she worked at Nordstrom. I respected her immensely.

Which leads me to the topic of managers—I had friends who would go through two or three managers in a year. Their departments were always in flux. I reached into the manager grab bag only four times in ten years, which must be a record. What's even more amazing is that each time I pulled one out, I got a winner.

My second manager didn't beat around the bush either. She taught me a lot about becoming a manager, treating people with respect, and team-building. She went to Ireland for three months to fill in for someone on leave. When she returned, she brought with her a wonderful tradition of tea time. Every day, the team would go to the cafeteria for 15 to 20 minutes and chat. It doesn't sound like much, but in those 15 minutes a day, we got to know one another and we became a team, which made working together a whole lot more effective.

I loved being involved in the international aspect of the products. I watched, listened, and learned. Eventually, I broke out of admin work and steadily climbed up into middle management, still working on localization projects. I managed the process that took the English-language printed books and Help files and got them translated into a variety of languages.

The International group was like a different world at MS. I would hear any number of languages being spoken in the halls by all the foreign nationals working on our localized products. I'd never been exposed to so much culture (hell, I'd never been out of the U.S.), and I ate it up.

The best part of the job (besides the free pop of course) was the dress code, which could be described as "What dress code?" My aunt was wrong. I didn't have to wear nylons and a skirt. In fact, I donned jeans, T-shirts and sweatshirts on a daily basis. Most of the shirts were, in fact, Microsoft issue. I wore the product shirts I was awarded with great pride. Today, I'm hard pressed to find anything in my drawer that doesn't sport a Microsoft logo.

It was a perfect fit for me, as I'm myself in jeans and a T-shirt. I'd visit my friends' million-dollar homes and their closets didn't hold the formal wear, sports coats and stuffed shoe racks you'd expect for people of their means, but rather piles of sweatshirts, jeans, and tennis shoes.

As my role grew, so did my responsibilities, and with that came world travel. Over the years, I traveled to many countries all over the world. Each place opened my eyes to the differences in the world and cultures and it also showed me how we're really all alike.

China was the biggest culture shock to me. I was overwhelmed by the crowded, filthy streets and the lack of sanitation. I couldn't believe the tiny apartments people lived in or how much control the government had over their private lives. The first day there, we entered a run-down building with one unisex bathroom for all five floors. The conference room didn't have a single chair that had all its casters, so we all sat lopsided through the meeting. The window next to the door was broken. Power and phone service were intermittent.

Still, I sat at a table with the warmest people I've ever met. I opened my daytimer (which was attached to me like a third hand) and started taking notes. One of the women noticed the pictures I always carried of my two children. Instantly, all the women in the room flocked to where I was sitting and started chattering in Chinese and pointing to the pictures. Finally, I was able to break in and ask what all the fuss was about. They were trying to imagine what it would be like to have the good fortune to have not one, but two children.

I climbed the Great Wall and saw the Summer Palace and the Forbidden City. I also saw the pyramids and the Sphinx, watched Germans put up a Maypole during a town celebration, and fought with airport officials in Kuwait over not being allowed to leave the airport because I was an "unaccompanied" woman. I've been questioned by airport security in Tel Aviv, walked the farmers markets in Seoul, ridden the world's fastest elevator in Yokohama, kissed the Blarney Stone and on and on all because of Microsoft.

After a few years, the International group was dissolved. The powers-that-be decided that it would be better to have the internationalization work done right in the U.S. groups. My new manager knew nothing about localization, the perfect scenario for me. I got to teach him, which meant things were done the way I wanted them to be done.

Over the years, he took *very* good care of me. He more than doubled my salary in those years. He even gave me the extremely rare and coveted 5.0 rating. This was the best review rating possible and it had to be approved by the company President.

We were a great team. I told him what I thought and he supported me. Over the years, we argued a lot, not about work, but about politics. We were on opposite ends of the spectrum. The good thing about our political debates was that he did make me think of things in different ways. He was the most well-read person I'd ever encountered and a bit of a history buff, which made debating with him quite challenging. When he decided to retire, it left a big hole to fill.

Which brings me to my fourth and final manager at Microsoft. He was harder to get to know and so we never developed the kind of rapport I'd had before, yet he was supportive and let me run my group the way I wanted. If you ask anyone, managers can make or break you.

When I first joined the domestic Windows NT writing team, I was astonished at the people I was interacting with on a daily basis. I remember the amazement I felt when I walked into a Barnes & Noble bookstore and saw a book written by one of my co-workers on the shelf. I was surrounded by excellence. There's no other way to describe it.

It wasn't all work and no play. We worked hard, yes. It was stressful to be sure, but it was so worth every minute. How could one not excel and want to succeed in this environment? And that's what it was all about—Microsoft really let you go and achieve and as long as you brought results, you were rewarded.

The job wasn't without frustrations. We worked continuously with a serious lack of information. Product plans changed by the minute. Features were added or removed and there was no time to communicate it properly. Half of my job involved just trying to figure out what the plan for the day was and how it affected my team's work.

I find it humorous when competitors claim that MS has some grand advantage and say, for example, that the Office team can work closely with Windows development to gain an unfair advantage.

The fact is, the groups don't communicate nearly enough. It's hard to find out what's happening on your own product, let alone what is going on with another product. That's one area where MS really falls short. The wheel is reinvented daily because people are spread too thin to look around and see what's happening in other areas of campus.

This lack of communication really reared its ugly head in respect to the tools we used to manage our documentation projects. We were always tweaking, putting on band-aids and struggling to keep up with technology. Every group did things differently, which made it impossible to share tools and processes. I kept trying to imagine what our external partners must go through as they worked with all of us. In practice, working with Microsoft was like working with many different companies.

Another huge area of frustration came twice a year at review time when managers were put to a nearly impossible task. The message to the masses was that you set goals and were measured based on your success at meeting (or better yet, beating) those goals. The reality was that you were measured against your peers.

As a manager, you were doing your job if you got rid of deadwood and hired excellence. But our mandate was to give ratings based on a curve. A certain percent of our group had to receive a 3.0 rating, which was in people's minds like getting a C or even a D in school. Human Resources sold 3.0s as "meeting expectations," and said that there was nothing wrong with that rating.

Then they would turn to management and tell us that our job was to get people with 3.0s up to higher ratings. So, the catch is that if we did that, who was supposed to get a 3.0?

It almost made me want to go out and hire 3.0s so that I wouldn't have to punish the excellent staff I had by giving a 3.0 to someone who deserved a higher rating. As a manager, this policy drove me crazy and it created unnecessary competition in a group I was trying to get to work as a team.

The other part of the job that was nuts was budgeting. Each spring we'd run around and try to figure out what projects would be done in the next year. We always knew the big project we'd be working on, but there were also 30 to 40 smaller projects to manage every year. I would survey everyone I could think of and come up with a list, then compare it to what others had. Nowhere was there an upper manager saying, "These are the projects this division will work on over the next 12 months."

After I had a list, I would have to try to guess how large each project would be and when it would ship. I became a great fiction writer through this process. The fun part would come when I would submit my millions of dollars in localization expenses and then upper management would push back and say it was too much.

I finally learned to tell them to cut whatever they wanted. If I ran out of money, they wouldn't say, "Oh, well, we won't have a German version of Windows." I could always go back to my original numbers and say that they cut it, not me. Although it took years to achieve this confidence in my abilities, it felt good.

Over time, it became clear to my husband and me that he didn't have to work to make ends meet. This opened a whole new chapter in our lives. My husband quit his job so that he could accommodate my travels by being there with our kids. My job was too demanding to have both of us working long hours in high-stress careers. As we watched the stock grow and split and grow and split, we started dreaming about what we'd do after Microsoft.

When I came to MS, I never dreamt that I would become a millionaire in the process of working at a job I loved. I was, after all, an English major from a nothing school in the middle of nowhere who started working as a secretary. But then again, I also never imagined that the 2,500-person company I joined would grow to be the world leader it is today.

I had a hard time thinking of leaving. While the average burnout seemed to be at about five to seven years, I was still thriving on the adrenaline. My identity was so wrapped up in Microsoft that it was impossible to imagine not being there. When I had my kids, I had a hard time taking the standard three-month maternity leave. I was on email every day, went in for meetings, and even took my infant daughter to an all-day offsite meeting. I was addicted.

My husband and I agreed that we eventually wanted to move back to the Midwest to be closer to our families and to raise the kids in a small-town environment. The big question we couldn't agree on was when to make the move. Every time I came home after a stressful day and started complaining, he would remind me that I could quit tomorrow. That was something I didn't even want to think about doing, yet there was a certain peace of mind in knowing that I could.

For the next few years, we watched our friends build their dream homes. We stayed in our modest home because we knew that we would eventually move and would build our dream house then. My husband became more and more restless.

I was in the thick of what was then Cairo, or Windows NT 5. I'd been working on this project since its inception and took great pride in it. The team I led was amazing. The problem was, the years flew by for me, and still Cairo didn't ship. Cairo turned into Windows 2000.

My husband kept asking me when I wanted to leave. I kept saying, "As soon as we ship." As the product deadlines slipped farther and farther out, it became more and more difficult to wait to make our move. These "slips," as they were called, became a kind of torment to both of us.

As the project grew, so did my kids. But summer came and the project wasn't finished. I had to choose between my family and the project I'd lived and breathed for so many years. I chose my family and left in July, before Windows 2000 shipped.

It released in December and I was a major grump that week. There's something about the culture at MS that gets in your blood. It becomes as much a part of your life as your family—which could explain the high divorce rate among Microsofties.

Mary

✦

People look at me now, age 34 and retired, and they shake their heads. People think that once you have money, finances are no longer an issue. When my husband and I graduated from college and got married, we were so in debt I didn't think we'd ever get out of our financial hole. But once you do, you just start dealing with different issues.

The kinds of problems we now face have to do with how to raise kids so they don't become lazy bums or snotty rich kids. How do we teach them the value of hard work when, while we might be working very hard on our farm, we aren't actually working for a paycheck anymore? How much should we help the kids with college, how do we structure their trust funds so they won't go and blow it all? We worry about the jealousy our friends and family might feel towards us as they go off to their nine-to-five jobs as they will until they're 65.

The question for us will be how it affects our friendships and family relations over time. At this point, we've been keeping a low profile and many people don't realize our situation. But we do have friends who know the scoop and who are jealous. For example, a good friend of mine really put my life in perspective when he reminded me, "Your big life decision now is which piece of dirt you're going to build your mansion on."

I've had a rare opportunity to mingle with a lot of people with way too much money. Some go out and spend it as soon as they get it, some gamble it away, some hoard it. Me? I guess I'm a little on the hoard side. I still find myself shopping at Target or Wal-Mart. I'll go into the grocery store and buy the generic brand of cereal because it's fifty cents less. I still remember when I would *have to* wait for triple-coupon day to do my grocery shopping. Those days may be long gone in terms of where I am financially, but in my mind, they might as well have been yesterday.

Here in small-town America, the challenge is to live your life while trying not to stand out. People probably think we are selling drugs or something—how else could two people our age get by without working? Some people actually feel sorry for us because we haven't found jobs yet. They make suggestions as to where we might look. We try not to be too blunt about our wealth for obvious reasons, but it's an odd situation.

Since I retired seven months ago, in between large projects like renovating barns and adding on to our temporary house or planning our dream house, I fill my days with small things. I do the household chores. I run my kids here and there for school and other events, we bowl in a local league, I play in a jazz band and try to work out daily (something I never had time or energy to do when I was at Microsoft).

I guess the computer bug is still in me because I can't get through the day without checking my email several times. I love to keep in touch with all the people back at Microsoft and all my friends who have since moved on. And most importantly, I'm getting to spend some real time with my children. I see how they grow and change every day and I realize how much I missed while I was fighting over budgets and review ratings.

Others who left before me warned me that it would take six months to a year to get Microsoft out of my system. I miss the people and the work and sometimes I even long for the stress, but all in all, I am at peace with my new life.

It's funny though, I still dream about Microsoft almost every night. Often it's a simple dream where I'm at my desk in one of the dozens of offices I occupied over the years and I'm visiting with people I worked with, or I'm in a meeting solving imaginary issues in my sleep. They're sweet dreams.

Peter

Peter married early, right out of college, and made babies before some of his friends could even get a date. He's the kind who has plenty to say but might choose to observe a conversation for a while before joining in. He has dark hair, warm brown eyes, and a medium build. He wrote the first version of his chapter entirely in a numbered list. Did I mention geek yet? He has comments about priorities and choices, and he's not too sympathetic to those who made choices they later regretted.

I had a lonely childhood with few friends and spent all my time reading books like "A Boy's First Book of Electricity Experiments." In junior high school the other kids picked on me, I had no real friends, and I was so bored in school I constantly earned the comment "Peter's achievements do not match his ability." In high school, the other kids either beat me up or ignored me, with the exception of the small group of friends who also were either ignored or beat up.

When I was in 10th grade, I learned how to program computers. There was no turning back. I had horrible grades but stellar SAT scores. I got a job at Farmer's Bank working with computers and socked away money for college.

I went to college, studying computer science and statistics. At the orientation they told us that only one in three freshman entering the program would last a year. I looked at the two people on either side of me and thought, "Tough luck for you two." The next four years were a blur of no sleep, little food, and a lot of very long periods of very hard work. While I went to school I held down a job programming— probably fifty hours a week during the summer, and perhaps twenty during the school year.

I graduated and got a job at Bell Labs. The Bell system was being dismembered by Justice Green and the consent decree: no more Bell Labs, at least not like before. Before I left, I worked on operating system performance tuning and analysis, a fairly arcane field. Transfers from one department to another were frozen while they figured out who would go where. I was not particularly happy.

I started interviewing with a fair number of UNIX groups, mostly up and down the east coast. Most of the companies seemed either rigidly hierarchical or else hopelessly disorganized. I interviewed at one firm building UNIX graphics workstations and the first person I talked to was clearly drunk at about 9:30 a.m.

I responded to a job offer posting on Netnews (which was still in its infancy) put up by Microsoft. It turned out the lead for the job was a friend of a fellow I knew. My friend called the guy at Microsoft, introduced me, and we had a nice conversation, with the Microsoft guy inviting me out for an interview. I was stunned that Seattle was green in the middle of winter.

Microsoft had a policy then that either they made a job offer on the spot or you were history. I remember talking briefly with Steve Ballmer about representations of numbers in negative bases (pretty interesting, actually), and then he made the offer. After flying back to New Jersey and talking it over with my wife, we decided that there would never be a better time to make that sort of move. People at Bell Labs thought I was nuts. I turned down offers of substantially more money to go to Microsoft.

I did manage to get Steve to boost the offer by raising the starting salary. If I had had any sense at all, I'd have gotten him to double or treble the amount of stock—I suspect he'd have done that with less resistance than he put up over raising the salary.

When I accepted the job offer, the woman coordinating things asked me if there was anything unusual about my possessions that might make a difference in the move. I told her we had about a ton of books. She laughed. The estimator for the moving company came out, wrote up the estimate, and she saw it. It was a bit larger than she expected: the biggest item was boxing and transporting 2,000 pounds of books.

My wife Wendy had never been to Seattle, ever. I had told her that although it rained, it never rained hard. When we arrived at SeaTac airport, it was raining. It was raining hard, so hard that the big, fat raindrops were hitting the tarmac and splashing back up past the windows of the jet. It looked like it was raining both up and down. Wendy stared out the window, stunned, and the flight attendant leaned over and asked, "Are you finally home?" Wendy looked up at the flight attendant, back out the window, and then burst into tears.

✦

Was there more work than could be done? Yes. Were the hours long? Yes. Everyone wanted to be there, so it didn't seem to matter. At the age of 22, it didn't matter if you had a real life outside of work, because if you're the sort of person who would be attracted to Microsoft at that time, your life *was* your work anyway. One of the appealing things about Microsoft in the early days was that the vast majority of us wanted to be doing what we were doing, and getting paid for it was a nice bonus. The Xenix group was a wonderful group of people, and I was very happy.

A friend and I did the Xenix-386 port (I wrote the demand-paged memory management, he wrote everything else) and were thus the first people to run a native 386 operating system on the 386. It ran on a prototype machine built by Compaq, and you had to hose off the processor with Freon to keep it from overheating. I did a bunch of performance work on Xenix that helped close some business deals. I got called into so many meetings and was introduced with "This is Peter; he's our technical guy," that I had business cards that read "Technical Guy" for the job title.

I liked Microsoft, especially at the beginning, but unlike most of my co-workers, I was married and had something resembling a life outside of MSFT. As time went on, it became increasingly clear that eventually I'd need to make a choice between cutting back on my family time (especially after my first child was born) or cutting back on MSFT. MSFT lost. My particular choice was *not* the decision made by most of the people around me.

Some of my managers were fine with my insistence on having a home life while others were not. When I was in the Xenix group it didn't seem to be much of an issue. I'm sure I must have been asked to work the occasional weekend, but by and large my work went pretty smoothly and it was not a constant issue.

When I had people working for me I tried to make it clear that I didn't expect them to work weekends. Some did anyway. I sure hope they weren't trying to impress me because all it did was make me think that if they were really good they'd get their work done during the workweek.

In the Windows NT group my hours were more of an issue. At one point someone asked me to work one particular weekend, and I just said no. There was a long, long silence, and then he walked off. He was pretty clearly pissed, but what could he do, fire me? This is part of what I don't understand. If they ask you to work on a weekend, it means there's no one else who can do it. And if there's no one else who can do it, they can't do much to you, can they?

Maybe I'm just impervious to the "this won't be good for your career" pressure they expect to work. You've only got so much energy and attention to go around. Kids demand energy and attention. It's not as if you can negotiate whether you're going to pay attention to your kids. I don't understand why people have kids and then resent the fact that kids take up all their time and energy. What did they think was going to happen?

At some point along the way, the atmosphere at Microsoft started to turn toxic. There's not much point to bringing toxic stuff home from work; it's better to just try to leave it behind so that it doesn't suck you down.

✦

Putting my family first hurt my career. It certainly slowed my advance, and it certainly capped the highest point I could reach. When I left the 'Soft in 1994 there was no possible way I could have advanced to a higher level on the technical ladder without walking away from my commitments to my family and dedicating all my time to work.

I read the comments made by people who feel victimized by Microsoft: "Sure, I got five million dollars out of working at Microsoft, but I got divorced and I don't know my kids and I'm not happy. It wasn't worth it."

Give me a break. Every day, we get up and decide what to do with our lives. You can put the family first, or you can put the job first. They picked job and I picked family. They ended up with a stratospheric career and a dead-end family. I ended up with a wonderful family— wife and kids I love and who make every day worth living.

Our second child, Greg, while still an infant, managed to scald his feet with hot water one day. Wendy called me at work, but I was in another office. She left a careful message with all sorts of details about what the injury was, who was hurt, and where they were going for treatment. When I got the message from the MSFT phone operators, the message was "One of your children has been severely injured and you should go to the hospital immediately." If there was a traffic law I didn't break on the way to the hospital, I don't know what it might have been. It convinced me that my family was a lot more important to me than my job.

✦

Is Microsoft an arrogant company? Ha! Early during my time at Microsoft, I was in the Xenix group—something of a backwater relative to the mainstream of the company. So my experience might differ substantially from someone elsewhere in the company. Bear in mind that the corporate culture was substantially different in 1983 from what it was in 1994.

The Xenix group had, hmm, different ideas about code portability and other issues from a lot of the other people at Microsoft and even more so from the UNIX community outside the company. And, looking for a polite way to put it, we were probably not particularly reluctant to share our views of how things should be done with other people.

I guess we were both arrogant and obnoxious. At one point, the Xenix group had a nice motto. "Not arrogant; merely correct." It was not entirely a joke.

When we dealt with people outside the company, the Xenix group, being all young people, tended to focus entirely on outcome and very little on appearances. Not only did we not worry about how other people felt about the outcome, but perhaps there was even a hint of delight at being able to dictate technical decisions.

That didn't start to change until Paul Maritz came to the company and was, for a brief time, in charge of Xenix. Paul, being older, wiser, and far more mature and tactful, rapidly reeducated us, or at least tried. Paul described the Xenix group tactics as "Why use reason when force will do?" Okay, arrogant in a fairly major way.

✦

At one point in the middle of winter I was getting run down and depressed. I mentioned that I couldn't wait for spring to come. A whole bunch of folks turned this into one of the better pranks. The offices at Microsoft were reasonably spacious, but I made mine more so by keeping the furniture down to a file cabinet, two chairs, and a worktable (no desk). This left a fair bit of floor space.

So these folks pulled all the furniture out of my office, spread out plastic, then laid real, honest-to-God sod on the plastic. To make it like spring, they put in a golf tee (with ball), quite a few potted flowers, and put a tape of birdcalls on the stereo. They left a cigarette lighter and a note with lawn watering instructions: "Light lighter. Hold flame under sprinkler head."

Once word got out, I think damn near everyone at Microsoft strolled by to take a look. People called up spouses, who came to MSFT and brought the kids to come look. It was a fabulous prank but I got no work done for two days because people kept interrupting me to ask why I had sod in my office.

The best part is that the pranksters got the sod for free. When they went to the sod farm, the guy asked, "How much sod?"

"Just enough to cover the floor of a 9x12 office. How much?"

"It's free if you'll let me come and look."

The sod was down on the floor for maybe three days before it started to smell. The goons who laid it pulled it all up and put it in the main instigator's back yard to cover the spot where his dogs had dug holes.

When I started at MS, I had no idea about money. Well, maybe just a simple idea that if you earned more than you spent, you would end up with more than you started with. Wendy and I lived well below our means, ensuring that we kept the money invested rather than blowing it. We sold some stock to buy a minivan when Emily was born, and in retrospect that was a mighty expensive van.

We figured out that the stock would be worth something significant and set our sights on my retiring early. Our financial advisor told us our goals were impossible to achieve; I wanted to retire by 45. I was eager to get free of work before the kids were grown up. I would have gotten more stock if I had stayed longer but eventually you have enough. Yes, there really is such a thing as enough.

I worried about letting our lifestyle get too luxurious because it made retirement farther off. I called this tactic of keeping lifestyle costs low the Lifestyle Limbo—how low can you go? While I invested a lot of energy in work, I also invested a lot in figuring out exactly how much money I needed to retire. Projecting the stock option vesting forward made it look possible.

I had a little truck magnet that I used to hold things up on my whiteboard, which was gridded with one-inch squares. I started using the truck to mark off how many days I had left to go. Only one person figured out what was going on.

I left MSFT. I was 35. I wanted to call up our old financial advisor and say, "Neener, neener, neener."

People have a rather distorted idea of how much of an impact a given amount of money will have. There's a world of difference between an infinite amount of money and a million dollars. I'm okay with the attitudes of my family and friends, most of whom have some understanding. My neighbors think I'm pretty bizarre, but they'd probably think that regardless.

The rudeness of relative strangers when they find out you used to work at Microsoft (and so they assume you've gotten rich) is an annoyance. Everyone wants to know what I do. I tell them I'm a photographer or a writer or a consultant or something else plausible. Sometimes I tell them something that is calculated to shut down that line of conversation, for example, I say that I'm a xenophrenologist. About half of the people ask what that is. So far no one has continued that line of conversation after I tell them I make judgments about the personality of aliens based on their skull shape.

We got rich. But the story that got lost is that most of the people who got rich at Microsoft would have been successful people regardless. Maybe they wouldn't have found financial success, but they would have found real success—what really counts. They would have ended up with interesting lives, filled with challenges, and in the end they would have made the world a better place even if Microsoft had never existed.

I think it will be pretty interesting to see what those people go and do over the *next* twenty years. Already they're changing the face of American philanthropy.

✦

I started at Microsoft at the age of 24 and left at 35. I would have had to be dead to not learn some life lessons during that time. Still, my time at MSFT (and to a much lesser extent, Bell Labs) did teach me some important things I might not have learned elsewhere.

I thought I was a pretty competitive guy. Compared to some of the cutthroat competitors at Microsoft, I'm a non-competitive guy. Especially now, after most of the competition circuits in my brain have been fused into slag—I just don't have the killer instinct.

There are things that are worse than working for a bad manager. One of them is being a bad manager.

There's a sweet spot where the work you get paid for doing and what you need and want to do converge. When you're in that spot, there's a difference in how you approach the work, how it feels to do it, how it gets done, and the quality of the outcome.

I'm not a writer. Robert Frost was. He wrote:

> But yield who will to their separation
> My object in living is to unite
> My avocation and my vocation
> As my two eyes make one in sight.
> Only where love and need are one
> And the work is play for mortal stakes,
> Is the deed ever really done
> For Heaven and the future's sakes.

Truer words were never written.

You only get a finite amount of time. At the end of your life, you can't trade in the money for more time.

Doing something you hate, day after day, will kill you just as surely as getting shot in the head.

Life is not fair. Doing the work and getting the credit are not the same thing.

Success is not something you work towards—a goal. It's what you do every day: get up and be successful. Do what you love, love what you do. Work on what matters to you. Make the world better; fill your life with things that make you happy. Don't be afraid to tackle something big.

Look at the lives of the people you think are successful, the people you respect and admire. Look at the lives of people who have won a MacArthur, or a Pulitzer, or a Nobel Prize.

If you think that you don't want a life like the one most people have, if you want to be extraordinary in some way, you're going to have to be *different* from all those ordinary people. Don't be afraid to be different.

That said, being different just to be different is not much help. You have to be willing to take risks, to have people think you're crazy, but you also have to be working toward some plan. You have to take time to look at your life and see if it's heading in the direction you want. "The life unexamined is not worth living."

Asking whether it was worth it is a joke, right? I got to work at a nice place, in a nice, clean, safe office, on things I really enjoyed, with really smart people who by and large were my friends, and I got enough money that I don't need to work for pay any more, and even have enough to put some of it to use supporting charities I think are important.

Were there times I didn't like my job? Absolutely. Just before I left, I hated it so passionately I sometimes threw up while contemplating going to work. To ask if it was worth it doesn't even make sense. I'm profoundly grateful I had that period in my life. I managed to not self-destruct, came away with a stable marriage and two wonderful children. I live in one of the most beautiful regions on the planet, in a beautiful home. It's not a matter of "Was it worth it?" it's a matter of "Can I be grateful enough?"

While I was working at Microsoft, I watched people all around me run their lives into ruin, destroy their marriages and families, lose track of what was important to them, and blow all the money on toys. But there's a lot of difference between someone holding a gun to your head and saying, "Do this" and a company holding out a pile of money and saying, "Do this."

The question to ask the people who feel it wasn't worth it is this— when you felt like Microsoft was consuming your entire life, and your boss asked you to work on the weekend, did you ever, even once, just say no?

✦

Wendy and I bought a motor home. For the next four years, we took the kids and traveled for three months each summer. We visited every state in the continental U.S. and all the Canadian provinces except Newfoundland. We had a terrific time. We have a lot of fun. Our investments have done well. We bought some property and are building a new house. We're very active in our Quaker meeting. The kids talk to me about school because I'm right there. When they need help with homework I can help, because I'm right there. I did a bit of consulting. I didn't like it, so I stopped.

I'm doing photography, which I'd loved as a child, trying to put together a book on the transition between being a kid and being a young adult. I've got two more projects besides the book that I'm working on, one documenting the vanishing rural aspect of the Snoqualmie Valley and one that's a set of images on religious themes. I'm part of a group of photographers that meets every other week to review new work. I hung work in a bunch of group shows and put together a solo show.

I have never, not even for a fraction of a second, wished I had not left Microsoft. I sometimes wish I had left earlier. I'll look back on much of my time at Microsoft as some of the finest hours in my life. But there's a whole lot out there, things to see and do. Life post MS is great. To those who are afraid to leave, all I have to say is come on in, the water's fine.

Karin

For most of us, if you did the work you got the money. The money does change your life; for example, you suddenly have the luxury of saying things like "Money doesn't change things. It can't make you happy." Actually, it's true. Money doesn't make you happy, but it sure can make you more comfortable and it can change what you worry about.

The week I joined Microsoft in 1983, the company had grown to around 320 people. The recruiter gave me a big song and dance about the stock options, but my offer did not include any. It would be a couple years before I received any options, and then they were doled out to me with an eyedropper. My developer friends said that at the time the standard offer was between 1,500 and 2,000 shares to new graduates. I say "standard offer," but it wasn't, really. Some developers got more or got less or even got nothing.

My last boss loved to introduce me by mentioning how long I'd been with the company because it invariably provoked a reaction. Often the next question to me was "What are you still doing here?" the implication being that surely, in the years I'd been there, I'd made such a killing with my stock options that I could retire anytime.

Part of the answer was that I loved working at Microsoft and I wasn't ready to leave. Another part was that I didn't have as much money as people assumed—the granting of stock options was somewhat random, although the company tried various schemes to standardize it over the years. Bosses who weren't good negotiators for themselves or their groups didn't get as much stock to distribute, and then sometimes personal likes and dislikes rather than job performance influenced the distribution.

The best places to get lots of stock were upper management, marketing, or development. Documentation, where I worked, was not the hottest spot in the company. It was amazing, though, that the stock was granted throughout the company, uneven though it was. Microsoft was among the first to do this, and suddenly the tech-industry landscape changed.

Purely by lucky timing, tech largesse and the stock market combined to create a windfall for us. Certainly many, many jobs require long, hard hours—business owners, farmers, journalists, teachers, cops, parents—and don't get the same kind of financial payoff. Here we were, working no harder than many other people, yet we were being showered with money to do our jobs.

If you got stock in the first place, the trick was not to dump it right away. After we went public and our stock quickly climbed to $32 a share, a friend who's now the billionaire founder of another tech company told me to sell right away because we'd never be this high again.

Maybe I would have sold if I'd owned any stock. Actually, I did, a whopping 125 shares. Each employee was entitled to buy 250 shares at the initial public offering price. When we went public in 1986, I was still scrimping and saving to make it month to month, so my parents fronted me the money to buy the shares, keeping half of them. I sold about nine months later, thrilled to have made a thousand dollars. A *thousand* dollars, did you hear me? I was rich! They held out for about a year before selling, making twelve thousand.

A bittersweet game is to look at what you *could* have had. We all do it. We all sold, at least a little. For a while, the lure of the money is so mesmerizing you are unable to ignore it. After a few years of letting your hopes ride on the stock price, you learn to pull back, at least some of the time. It's crazy-making, as insubstantial as basing your happiness and self-worth on your looks or your job title or praise from others. You have to live by your own deepest values, rather than feeling good on days the stock is up and bad on days it's down. Easier said than done, unfortunately.

We are one mixed up culture when it comes to money. I don't know anyone who would turn down the cash if they won the lottery, yet we automatically believe that people who have money are insensitive, selfish, different. Other.

Suddenly here we were, watching our jobs turn into winning lottery tickets. I saw an awful lot of people look at their stock, see maybe thirty thousand dollars, and all they could think was *car, boat, trip...* So they'd sell their stock and buy that car. They couldn't wait. That thirty thousand didn't look like a nest egg or the potential to be more later, it looked like a car *now*. And we all could have used the money during those first years.

The seeds of how you handle money are planted early. Somehow, on the earnings of a schoolteacher and a contractor, my parents took the family of three girls to Mexico, Europe, Hawaii, and Alaska.

Then came the year when the water supply was too tight to allow new homes to be built in Santa Barbara, so we lived on mom's schoolteacher salary. The dishwasher broke, the car broke, and I heard fights through the bedroom wall about the bills.

I was fourteen, and would lie awake thinking about what I should do, what I could do, and how I never wanted to worry about money when I grew up. My sisters and I had savings accounts with little passbooks where we could see the totals increasing a few dollars at a time. Money went in, because that's what money was for, but it rarely came out.

So when I started working, I was careful. I always found cheap places to live, sharing houses and apartments with other people. I watched my budget. If I bought new $30 soccer shoes because I could feel the turf through the hole in my sole, I couldn't do anything else extra until the next paycheck. In spite of this penny pinching, I was still completely out of money every two weeks. It frustrated me, especially when Microsoft started a retirement plan and a plan for employees to buy company stock at a discount. I participated at the maximum rate for both the 401(k) and the employee stock purchase plan. For years after that my raises served only to get me back to where I'd been before the withholding started.

Now I was twenty-six, and I would lie awake thinking about how to juggle the few dollars in my bank account. Was there any chance I could find Jeanne and ask her for the $150 deposit she'd never paid me when she took over my room at college a few years before? I spent that $150 five ways every time I thought about it.

I got my first stock grant in 1985, and after a year or so, started dreaming about it. If the stock price doubled from the price I had to pay for it, I'd make $3,000. That sounded like an awfully big pile of money to me and I worried that I wouldn't do the right thing. And those seeds about doing the right thing, about never wanting to worry about money, had taken root long before.

I started reading about personal finance so I could figure out what to do with my $3,000 fortune. Using the calculator on my computer, I'd look at what I'd net if I sold my stock options right then. Then I'd multiply the profit by two, multiply it by two again, and again until it was a number I hardly dared imagine.

Waiting for the big payoff was excruciating. If you don't have a lottery ticket, you don't think about the lottery. If you do have a ticket, and you're watching lottery numbers being revealed and your ticket matches number after number, the tension squeezes you until you can barely breathe. And it took years, not seconds.

I especially felt pressure because this was my one chance. What extraordinary value did a technical editor/middle manager bring to a company? I was surrounded by developers, the hot property in the tech marketplace. They could go to another company or start their own and rake in the bucks. My degree in French and my experience with documentation didn't exactly seem like a ticket to the high life. I'm a worrier (I'm concerned about that), so for years I had a worry mantra running through my head.

Looking back, it seems like we should have known the payoff was coming. But as it was unfolding, there was no predicting that Microsoft was going to bust through record after record of performance and would take part in a huge, crazy run-up of the whole stock market.

How do smart guys from Harvard, Princeton, and MIT entertain themselves and make a little money? They form teams and play blackjack in Atlantic City. What do those smart guys do when they meet up in a place like Microsoft? They form teams and play blackjack in Las Vegas.

When a blackjack team formed at Microsoft, I was invited to join. We practiced together once a week and everyone had to pass a test, a checkout, every six months. We were trusting each other with large amounts of money and we had to prove that we could play perfectly under pressure.

At first I didn't actually count cards, I learned just the basic strategy where every possible combination of your cards and the dealer's card has a predetermined play. When we went to Las Vegas, my job was to talk with the pit bosses and the other players at the table, distracting them from the fact that my "date" wasn't saying much. Eventually I found that counting cards, even with a six-deck shoe, was more a matter of concentration and practice than anything else and I became a card counter.

Counting isn't illegal—we weren't cheating—but Las Vegas casinos are private property and they can toss you out if they don't want you there. Atlantic City casinos don't bother to throw you out, but they will shuffle the cards if they think you're counting. When they do that, you lose your advantage. I'm not sure who was fooling whom—maybe we thought we were being tricky and secretive while the casinos simply used our names and birth dates to look up information about us.

It helped to be female. If she curls her hair and wears lipstick, can she possibly be smart, too? I was usually treated paternally by the older male hosts and the pit bosses whose job was to watch the players for cheating and to decide who gets comped (meaning who they're going to give free dinner, free show tickets, free rooms, and so on). I'm sure at least some of them didn't believe a woman could possibly be counting six-deck shoes for hours at a time.

My first trip as a counter was a disaster. I'd played a number of times as the date, where the guy I was with was counting but I wasn't, and I loved to play. I was excited and nervous the first time I went out to count by myself and wanted to play even though the casino wasn't hopping. The more players there are at the tables, the harder it is for the casino to watch everyone. That was mistake number one.

Mistake number two: I was the biggest player at the blackjack tables that night. I was using stacks of $500 chips, and you can see their bright lavender color from a mile away. You attract attention from passersby, from pit bosses and hosts, and surely from the overhead surveillance people. Purple chips are nowhere near the highest, and playing a couple thousand dollars on a hand of blackjack is only starting to be big money, but my bets were big relative to the action at the tables that night. I didn't think about how much I was standing out.

Mistake number three: continuing to play at the same casino the following morning. I'd been playing only a little while when there was a tap on my shoulder.

"Would you pick up your chips and come with us, please?" a short man in a suit asked me. Two other men stood behind him.

"Why?" My heart started pounding.

"Would you come with us, please?" His face was grim.

Mistake number four: alarmed but unsure what else to do, I collected my chips and followed the three men into the back of the casino. They photocopied my driver's license. They backed me up against the wall and took my picture. They were gruff and serious and although they didn't physically or verbally threaten me, I was upset and on the verge of tears. They wouldn't tell me anything except that I was no longer allowed to play there, that I'd be escorted to my room, and then would have to leave the property immediately. If I returned, they'd arrest me for trespassing.

"I'm here with a friend. How am I supposed to let him know where I am?"

"You have to leave the property immediately."

A guard took me to my room and watched from the doorway as I packed. I left a note in the room for my teammate, telling him to meet me at the casino across the street for lunch. Within minutes I was out on the sidewalk with my suitcase. I crossed the street, went straight into the casino's bordello-red lounge, and tried to compose myself.

I felt horrible and when my teammate and I met up, we decided to go downtown and stay there for the rest of our weekend. Because I'd been caught, I'd jeopardized his status (would they assume we were both card counters?) and ruined our weekend. We were paid by the team to play; now we wouldn't make money for playing, nor would we be able to bring home any winnings. We also wouldn't be comped. But my teammate was terrific—he didn't blame me and was calm and kind about the whole thing.

When we got home, the team discussed the situation. We decided that we should refuse to go into any back rooms. If we were asked to, we should just hang onto the table and start yelling. We figured the casinos wouldn't want the fuss and would kick us out without taking us in the back.

After licking my wounds for a few weeks, I decided I wanted to try again. Security personnel at casinos use books of photos to know who should be thrown out, and I was crossing my fingers that my photo hadn't made it into the book. I worked harder to blend in. I played for several years after that and was never kicked out again.

Our team was uncommonly lucky and although we had some losing trips, more were winners. We came out substantially ahead every year for the four years I played on the team. We each kept careful track of our share of the winnings and of our salary for playing, and everyone declared the income on his or her taxes.

✦

The calculated risk-taking of blackjack had its effect on me. It led me into a stock market trading style I considered to be just like blackjack, except you didn't have to sit in a smoky casino. No doubt the fact that we kept winning at blackjack also influenced me. If we'd lost or had more disastrous trips, I probably wouldn't have become as aggressive a trader.

Friends of mine had been buying and selling MSFT for years, just counting on it bouncing around enough for them to make money as it bounced. It goes down and you buy it, it goes up and you sell it. Do that with a thousand shares and you make one or two thousand bucks. I decided to try it.

I guessed wrong on my first attempt, and lost money. A few years later when my brokerage account was heftier, I was ready to try again. I started by buying and selling MSFT, just like before. This time it worked. I'd call my broker (they didn't have online trading yet) and buy, call the next day and sell, and make a thousand dollars in a day. I'd then run out into the hallway at work and look for someone I could tell.

It was a thrill. It was a drug. And it was addictive. After a few trades, I was bringing in as much money as I did through my salary, but it took only minutes a day. Not so bad for Microsoft (the employer, not the stock), because the trading took one minute and the running around finding someone to tell took ten minutes. Eventually I learned to mostly keep my mouth shut about my trades, although at first it was overwhelming to be able to make money so easily. I also began selling puts and calls, which for a while, given the extreme upward trend of the market, was a profitable strategy.

It takes a certain personality to make money trading: you have to be willing to gamble yet not be a compulsive gambler. It also takes money to get started in trading. Maybe rich people have the big brokerage account necessary to get started, but they aren't going to be motivated to do the work to figure out a strategy.

The books on options trading are thick, technical, and full of formulas. I had the books and studied parts of them, but even though I was motivated I found them too excruciatingly boring to read in their entirety. I used simple strategies, made money on nearly all of my trades, and didn't worry about what I was missing by not reading further in my reference books.

Some days, watching stocks move, I could almost hear the market breathing. It was like a big animal, unbelievably powerful, with sharp claws and teeth, but if you could successfully ride on its back the thrill was amazing.

The game changed, as it always does, and between 1995 and 1999 a lot of the juiciness went out of options pricing. I did more short-term trading of stocks, going for that little bounce. That worked pretty well.

I knew I was on thin ice this whole time, though, because not only had MSFT exceeded all expectations, the market had too many years of exceptional returns. When the market outperforms, some poor performance is due so that the stock market can maintain its average return. But the addiction was powerful, and although I worried, I didn't stop. I made money year after year.

In 2000 it all caught up to me. I'd written a big check to my ex-husband for my divorce in February, adding to my debt at the brokerage. My ex and I had developed a dangerous lifestyle using margin debt (borrowing against the value of my stocks) to pay for new cars, landscaping for the new house, to pay huge tax bills from my trading gains and from selling MSFT, and on and on. All summer long and into December I was getting margin calls, where the value of the assets I was holding had sunk too low to sustain the loans I'd taken out. I was forced to sell many tech stocks at a loss, and forced to sell MSFT at a third of its high.

This tech stock crash has taken away my safety net—mine and millions of other people's. I feel for the people who've lost their retirement accounts and don't have much time to recover. Making financial decisions is annoyingly stressful because you have only conjecture and assumptions to base a decision on. The more you study and read, the more dissenting opinions you'll hear, making decisions more difficult. You can quickly get a grasp on conventional wisdom, but when you dig deeper, there are plenty of smart people who advocate something a little different. Then what do you do?

Who can say exactly how the market, and MSFT, will do in the next few years? Or long term? If you choose the wrong path, you jeopardize your financial future. The stakes are so high.

Yet the path is always treacherous in one way or another. Microsoft was one of the first companies to share the wealth with virtually every employee, and we had no roadmap, no example to follow.

What we did depended on our own frailties or strengths. If you dumped your stock right away, no one could fault you for following conventional wisdom. But if you sold early, you did not get wealthy, or did not get anywhere near as wealthy as you could have if you'd waited. So employees at Microsoft, Cisco, Dell, Intel and the other behemoths of the industry got richest by holding on and waiting for the run-up. Waiting required either a willingness to take risk or a fear of or disinterest in money.

When the dot.com craze came, they followed our roadmap: the way to wealth was to hold on to that stock. Oops. By then the game had changed and the only way to keep any dot.com money was to get out early, before the roof caved in.

✦

Being at Microsoft puts you in a strange place: you end up with more money than people who didn't participate in the tech boom, but you see how wealthy some Microsoft people became, and it's easy to not feel rich. That's very, very warped.

We live in a country where even those who live paycheck to paycheck are already wealthy by world standards. Having a full refrigerator and a safe place to live is a miracle in itself. Yet it's easy, if you live paycheck to paycheck and have nothing set aside, to feel that you aren't well off.

And if you want to revel in having money, you'll have to tune out the fact that rather than retiring young, you could use your money to help the environment or to keep a homeless family fed and off the street for at least a while.

That's a complicated issue, though. I've learned the hard way that just giving money to someone who's struggling doesn't solve his or her problems. Sometimes—and I'm not saying all the time—people are in desperate straits because they make poor decisions at every turn. If they've given up hope and stopped taking responsibility for their choices, getting their hands on your money doesn't help them. The answer to helping other people involves more work and more thought than simply writing checks.

Seeing the full scope of need in the world is so overwhelming that you have to make your choices about where and how you can help. It sounds funny to say, but giving away money is not as simple as it seems.

Seattle has a good number of philanthropists: there's old money here, timber and real estate developers, and new money from McCaw Cellular, and Amazon (oops, hope you cashed out a while ago), and from that little software outfit, Microsoft.

The founder of Aldus, another software company, wanted to apply his entrepreneurial skills to the nonprofit sector. He founded a group called Social Venture Partners, which gives away money and places volunteers in the groups who receive it. SVP has caught on in other cities and is growing quickly. The nonprofit groups are the experts at the problems they're working on, whether it's an after-school program or the environment, and SVP helps them strengthen their business expertise: raising money, using technology, marketing their programs.

Money isn't the whole answer, but the people I see are giving their time and money to try to solve problems, hard ones. *That's* what is considered worthwhile. Sound familiar? It's smart people coming together in the community, the Microsoft way, and I'm left with hope.

✦

There *is* life after Microsoft. It didn't seem like there would be, sometimes. It was too intense, too all-consuming to be able to walk away and not feel itchy about leaving. One of the surprises for me was that it was so wonderful to have a life after Microsoft—after all, I'd spent nearly my whole working life there, my friends were there, my ties and self-image and daily routine all revolved around the place. I was, to put it mildly, attached.

Microsoft was the place I made the most friendships and friendly connections and came to know hundreds of co-workers. Yet leaving wasn't so bad, it didn't end the connectedness. An incredible community of Microsoft people still surrounds me.

It's a wonderful feeling to stay relaxed on Sunday evenings. To not feel wistful at the end of a weekend, to not dread the coming rush of the workweek.

I think one of the greatest gifts of not having to work for someone else is waking up on your own schedule. No alarm clocks. It's amazing to wake up because of the sun or because your body is fully rested and ready to go. Sometimes I feel like I'm swimming through time. There's a delicious richness to having enough time to do what you want.

Now, in our lives after Microsoft, we face our own demons. We have no excuses. There's no *I'm too busy at work; if only I had the money to go back to school.* Only our own weaknesses stand between us and our dreams. We have to take full responsibility for the course of our lives. It can feel awfully naked with no excuses to hide behind. The richness of having enough time sometimes turns into feeling as if it doesn't make any difference if you wait a little longer before turning to the activities that really matter to you. Time slips away from you and you have to force yourself to pay attention to your priorities.

Karin

✦

My former co-workers' reactions to being retired split cleanly in two: those who go on to the adventures we all imagine we'd want, and those who arrange a quiet, fun life with a small orbit.

I learned to rock climb in Utah recently. The brawny friend of a friend who taught me to climb quizzed me on my life, and I thought I could hear unspoken amazement that I didn't do more with my time. He works hard all week and spends his evenings and weekends having outdoor adventures with his wife. They rock climb, kayak, camp, hike, mountain bike, and ski like maniacs. I could feel his envy at the thought of not having to ration time for his adventures.

It's a very strange thing to have the time and the money to do as you want. When you're dreaming of the day you might have that, you can think of a million things to do. When it's your reality, you might not make the same choices you dreamed of. It's easier to stay home and travel a little than to spend a year or two on the road; it's easier to do what you're familiar with than to turn your life upside down.

Freedom is a gift and an opportunity. If I'm not rock climbing on a cliff in Borneo or sipping kir on the French Riviera, am I wasting the gift? I use my time to work on projects of my own choosing: a little stock options trading, my textile and mixed media art, and this book. It's mostly a quiet, fun life with a small orbit.

Maybe staying home rather than going to Borneo is partly age related. When we're younger, we seek adventure outside. We want to run around and see and feel and experience. Later, we want to nest more, and both the pleasures of home and the adventures are attractive.

Yet plenty of adventures are found by going within, no matter where you are. I'm looking forward to the next bend in the road.

Note

So there you have it, a few of the voices of Microsoft. Making a neat and tidy package out of this set of lives in progress is impossible: loose ends and messy bits poke out, and our stories change each day. A book is a snapshot. As soon as the snapshot is taken, people move on.

I'm insatiably curious about the end of any story. I want to know the outcome of snippets of talk I hear: was the baby healthy? Did they move to Europe?

If you're like me, you may have questions about the people whose stories you've just read. Pennington Books has a Web site where you can find out the end of the story, or at least the next chapter. I can't guarantee that everyone in the book will be willing to answer questions you send in, but most likely you'll be able to find out what you want to know.

If you have a question or a comment, please feel free to take a look at the Web site at www.penningtonbooks.com and send email.

Appendix

The Appendix contains three parts: the topics I sent to people to get the book started, a glossary, and a timeline that provides a little context for the chapters.

Here the topics, verbatim, from my original email that started off with "Want to participate in something that will make a more interesting memento of Microsoft than a T-shirt?" You can see that people chose which questions they wanted to answer, and a few exceptionally cooperative people answered them all.

1   Getting hired, getting to MS/moving to Seattle, first day, first weeks, learning curve.

2. The work load. The work.

3. Pranks. Funny stories. Microsoft culture. Is MS an arrogant company?

4. Personal life: early, mid, and late MS career, post MS.

5. The bucks. Did you get stock? Did you keep it? Did you have to learn about money? Was it important or minor to you? You don't have to answer these particular questions, they're to give you

things to think about. You may have an instant reaction to the topic of the money with your own points you want to make.

6. The bucks and your family/friends/neighbors. What kind of reactions did your parents, siblings, spouse, kids, and friends have? Did they make assumptions about you?

7. Life lessons learned. Was it worth it?

8. Your overall view of working at MS. Your overall view of technology, the tech industry, or whatever part of this experience makes you get on your soapbox.

9. How's life post MS? Here's your chance to send a message to the world. What is success? What would you do differently? What would you like to encourage kids or adults to do? Do you have any comments about time (how you use it, how much you have, can money buy time)?

10. Do you have another topic you'd like to mention? Please feel free to write about any aspect of working at MS.

Glossary

Jack, whose chapter appears early in the book, wrote the technical definitions.

API—Application Programming Interface. The interface that programmers use to manipulate something; for example, an operating system. The user interface is the interface that users use to manipulate something. Not all programs have a user interface, and not all programs have an API. Some have both. (The term API used to refer to the programming interface that applications use to talk to the operating system, but it's now a more general term.)

App or **Application**—A program such as a spreadsheet or word processor that performs a primary service for the user.

Calling in rich—Like calling in sick, but you have too much money to come to work.

Code—Verb or noun, to program a computer or a computer program: I coded for ten hours today. The code I wrote is good.

Compiler—A tool that programmers use. The compiler translates code written in a high-level language such as Fortran, Pascal, C, or C++ to something the computer itself can run, which is known as machine language. When humans write in machine language, most of the work consists of managing a lot of nitty-gritty details, most of which can be easily abstracted and have very little relevance to the big problem the programmer is trying to solve, so the early translation programs became known as "compilers" of those details. Modern compilers do a lot more than compile, but the name is still used. Today, nearly all programming is done with compilers and many professional programmers have never written a line of machine language, where in the early days, that was the only way coding could be done.

DEC—Digital Equipment Corp.

DLL—Dynamic Link Library. A library is a way of packaging small program fragments (called subroutines) so they can be used by a number of programmers. With a DLL, the library is a separate component from the program. One of the biggest innovations of Windows was that it was built almost entirely of DLLs. It was not the first system to do this, but it was the first to be highly commercially successful, which resulted in a host of complications its predecessors had not encountered.

Documentation—Instruction manuals for the software.

DRI—Digital Research, Inc. Formerly Intergalactic Digital Research, a name that reveals the extreme stuffiness of the software industry.

DSR—Dynamical Systems Research, a tiny company acquired by Microsoft.

Grant—Stock grant, meaning a commitment from Microsoft to allow you to buy a certain number of shares at a set price. For example, if you were granted 1000 shares at the price of $50 and a few years later the stock had split several times, you might be eligible to buy 8000 shares at $6.25.

GRE—Graduate Record Exam. A test required for entrance to graduate school in the United States.

HP—Hewlett-Packard Company.

HR—Human Resources.

IT—Information Technology.

Kludge—A quick and dirty way of doing something that is unaesthetic or inelegant from a programmer's perspective. Rhymes with huge. A hack is a quick and dirty way of doing something, no aesthetics implied. Some hacks are beautiful, some are kludges. Some kludges are efficient, some horribly inefficient. Kludginess, hackishness, and efficiency are unrelated (or as we say, orthogonal). A hacker is a person who hacks, that is to say, writes programs quickly off the top of his/her head. A cracker is a person who breaks into computers. Many hackers have done some cracking, but very few have devoted more than a little time to it. A cracker who intentionally causes any sort of damage is called a vandal. Causing damage, intentional or not, is a very serious violation of the hacker ethic and is considered a sign of incompetence, stupidity, or malice, all of which are unwelcome in the hacker community. Unfortunately, a few of the early crackers incorrectly called themselves hackers, and the media has picked it up. [Whew. Now you know what a kludge is, and you have a taste of what it's like to ask a question of a detail-oriented programmer.]

Lake Bill or **Lake Billg**—A pond between buildings on the Redmond campus.

Library—See DLL.

Localization—Making a product appropriate for a particular language and culture. Not only is the product translated into, say, Swedish, but examples will reflect Swedish customs.

Machine—Computer.

Margin Loan—A loan provided by your stock broker. Your broker uses the value of stocks you own as collateral. These loans are dangerous because if the value of your stock falls, your collateral is worth less and you may be forced to give your broker cash or to sell stocks to maintain the value of your collateral.

MS—Microsoft.

MSFT—The stock symbol for Microsoft, also used informally to refer to the company.

OEM—Original Equipment Manufacturer. The term is used in various industries; for Microsoft, OEMs are makers of computers.

OS—Operating system, such as Windows or MS-DOS.

OS/2—An operating system jointly developed by IBM and Microsoft. Eventually the partnership fell apart and IBM carried on alone.

Platform—The stable environment an application sees. It may be a microprocessor, an operating system, or a version of an operating system.

Pointer—A mechanism for making one datum point to another in memory. This is used for many data structures, including trees: each node contains one or more pointers to branch or leaf nodes.

Port—To modify a program to run on a different platform. For example, if Microsoft Word runs on the Mac, it can then be ported to run on Windows.

Program—Verb or noun, to program a computer or the computer program.

Regression—When a program is running smoothly, programmers keep careful track of how it's behaving. Sometimes, something you did to the program damages it, and its behavior "regresses" (although it's not always a step backwards; sometimes it goes off into new, wrong territory). By keeping a careful and detailed log, you can often figure out which change caused which regression. This is a very important testing tool.

Reorg—Reorganization. Some reorgs were small, and changed the reporting structure of a single group. Others were huge realignments of resources intended to reflect a refocusing of the entire company. Your project and your working relationships could be ripped apart again and again, year after year.

Rest and vest—Slang for continuing to work at Microsoft while making minimal effort; hanging on to continue collecting stock.

Review—Every year employees' performance is evaluated. On a scale of 1 to 5, a rating of 3.0 meant you were doing your job. At the same time, managers were encouraged to get their employees to rate above a 3.0, so no one considered it an acceptable rating.

Trace—A debugging technique that involves carefully following the actions of whatever's being debugged, typically a program.

Tree—A hierarchical structure for organizing data. It metaphorically resembles a tree, with a root, branches, and leaves.

Trekkie—Fans of the TV show Star Trek.

User Ed—User Education, the groups at Microsoft that wrote the instruction manuals. Also called documentation groups.

Vest or **Vesting**—Becoming eligible to buy stock in a grant. A grant becomes buyable, or vests, over time.

Vulture capitalist—Roger's personal slang for venture capitalists.

Xenix—Microsoft's version of UNIX, an operating system.

Xerox PARC—Xerox had a Palo Alto Research Center that pulled together a team of researchers who had invented the mouse, various aspects of the graphical user interface, and other innovations. They showed their ideas to companies including Apple, Microsoft, Sun Microsystems, IBM, and others. Apple later sued Microsoft for "copying" Apple's graphical user interface, the concept that Xerox's team had pioneered. Apple and Microsoft both made a bit of money off the concept, while Xerox's products never went anywhere.

Timeline

This information is compiled in part from the Microsoft Web site, a document called "Key Events in Microsoft History" provided by the Microsoft Museum, and from the book *The Making of Microsoft*.

1975—A new machine, the MITS Altair, appears. There's no screen or keyboard, so data input and output is for the hardcore only. Paul Allen and Bill Gates decide to write BASIC for the Altair.

1976—Bill Gates writes an infamous letter published in Computer Notes called "An Open Letter to Hobbyists." He chastises hobbyists for not paying for software. Microsoft officially becomes a company, based in New Mexico.

1977—Microsoft's five employees produce $500,000 in sales; $100,00 per employee.

1979—The company moves to Bellevue, Washington. Paul and Bill are from Seattle, so they're coming home. 25 employees produce $2.5 million in sales.

1980—Steve Ballmer, who actually graduated from Harvard, joins Microsoft. 40 employees produce $8 million in sales.

1981—IBM introduces its personal computer. 125 employees produce $16 million in sales.

1982—The first subsidiary is created in England. 200 employees produce $34 million in sales.

1983—Microsoft Word ships. Subsidiaries are established in France and Germany. 383 employees produce $69 million in sales.

1984—MS is the first software company to exceed $100 million in sales, with 608 employees producing $125 million in sales.

1985—Microsoft Windows ships. Version 1.0 is barely noticed, yet we continue to work on the product until we get it right. This tenacity, coupled with Microsoft's unusual ability to change direction quickly, make a tough combination to beat. All that change is hard on employees, though, as the preceding chapters make clear. 910 employees produce $140 million in sales.

1986—Microsoft goes public. The new stock symbol is MSFT. We move to our new world headquarters: four buildings where we'll all be together. We quickly outgrow the four buildings. 1,200 employees produce $197 million in sales.

1987—Tiny Microsoft and big IBM announce their joint development of OS/2. MSFT splits 2-for-1, meaning stockholders receive an additional share for every share they hold. Nearly 2,000 employees produce $300 million in sales.

1988—2,800 employees produce $590 million in revenue.

1989—4,000 employees produce revenue of $803.5 million. Over half the earnings come from sales outside the United States. One reason for Microsoft's success and reach: it went for international markets earlier than many other companies and stuck with them in spite of the many hurdles.

1990—Microsoft Windows 3.0 ships. It took five years, but we got it. MSFT splits 2-for-1. 5,200 employees produce $1 billion in sales.

1991—MS becomes one of the first software companies to undertake computer science research. MSFT splits 3-for-2. Stockholders receive an additional share for every two shares they hold. 9,631 employees produce $1.85 billion in revenue.

1992—MSFT splits 3-for-2. 12,452 employees produce $2.78 billion in revenue.

1993—Microsoft Windows is now the most popular graphical operating system in the world with more than 25 million licensed users. (How many unlicensed?) 14,430 employees produce $3.79 billion in revenue.

1994—MSFT splits 2-for-1. 15,017 employees produce $4.71 billion in revenue.

1995—Microsoft and NBC become equal partners in a 24-hour news channel and an online news service on the Microsoft Network. 17,801 employees produce $6.08 billion in revenue.

1996—MSFT splits 2-for-1. Microsoft announces ActiveX tools for creating Internet and PC content. Slate, an online magazine covering politics, culture, and public policy, appears on the Internet. 20,561 employees produce $9.05 billion in revenue.

1997—Microsoft invests $150 million in Apple. Internet Explorer 4.0 is shipped. 22,232 employees produce $11.94 billion in revenue.

1998—MSFT splits 2-for-1. 27,055 employees produce $15.26 billion in revenue.

1999—MSFT splits 2-for-1. 31,575 employees produce $19.75 billion in revenue.

2000—Microsoft stock plummets along with the market. 39,170 employees produce $22.96 billion in revenue.

2001—48,030 employees produce $25.3 billion in revenue.

2002—The company will not be ordered to split in two; MSFT rises. 50,621 employees produce $28.37 billion in revenue. The per-employee revenue figure is now $560,400, as compared to $100,000 in 1977. Those first three subsidiaries established in 1982 and 1983? They have company: 78 countries have Microsoft offices now, including Uruguay, Namibia, and Tunisia.

PENNINGTON BOOKS

Thank you for buying *Microsoft in the Mirror*.
We appreciate your order.

Would you be willing to help us out?

- We're looking to spread the word on this book and
  the upcoming management how-to book, so please
  tell a friend how to find us on the web at
  www.penningtonbooks.com.

- Do you know a TV, radio, or print journalist you
  could connect us with? Let us know via phone or

We hope you enjoy *Microsoft in the Mirror*.

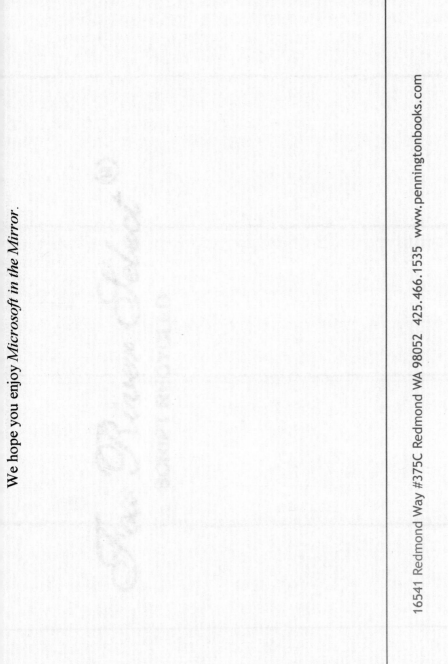

16541 Redmond Way #375C Redmond WA 98052 425.466.1535 www.penningtonbooks.com